A TRUE STORY OF INNOCENCE AND BETRAYAL

ANN NOVICK

Behind
PRISON
WALLS

MEKOR PRESS

Mekor Press, Inc.
© 2015 by Menucha Publishers
Typeset and designed by Gittel Kaplan
All rights reserved

ISBN 978-1-61465-127-7

Published and distributed by:
Mekor Press
A division of Menucha Publishers, Inc.
250 44th Street
Brooklyn, NY 11232
Tel/Fax: 718-232-0856
www.menuchapublishers.com
sales@menuchapublishers.com

Printed in Israel

This book is dedicated to my friend
Rose
Who held my hand
From the beginning

And to N.L.
For his constant caring, concern, and love;
And without whom this entire mess may have never ended.

A.N.

Contents

Author's Note

This memoir is based on a true story. It is compiled from my memories and others' recollections of the events, when they occurred and how they were experienced. The names and places have been changed. The letters are as they were written except for editorial changes.

A friend had called this event and its offshoots a parenthesis. It had a beginning and would have a definite end. It was set aside from the rest of our lives, having something to do with it but separate, unrelated, different, and horrible.

This is a story about a young woman's strength and courage. It is a story told through letters of introspection, growth, and responsibility. It is a story of faith in the face of terror. In sharing it, I hope it gives others strength in their time of adversity, as it did for me.

Please note: A glossary of foreign terms appears in the back of this book.

Special thanks to Doreen Glazer for her caring assistance with editing and feedback so that the book would be just right.

Tears of Joy

1

$\mathcal{I}$ watched my daughter, Miriam, look lovingly at her new husband, Daniel, and tears of joy ran down my face. They hated to be parted from each other even for a moment, even for the dancing.[1] Just married, they were so happy and full of joy.

I was living every mother's dream. As I reached into my purse for tissues to dry my eyes, my hand brushed against the tiny fridge magnet my daughter had bought for us in the little gift shop on the highway.

We had been on the road for three days. We had agreed to make the wedding in New York where the bride and groom lived and attended school. Our family and most of their friends lived there. It meant a long trip for us, but we were a family that loved road trips. "Parents hold their children's hands for a while, but their hearts forever" was the magnet's message. I vowed I would keep it close to me always. Life could not get better.

I watched Reuben, my husband, and Miriam do a *mitzvah tantz*. A

---

1. At religious Jewish weddings, the room is divided as men and women do not dance together.

9

long chain of napkins tied together connected them as they moved in a circle. My husband was having trouble keeping his wheelchair out of the way. He laughed each time the napkins got caught in his wheel. My daughter lovingly helped him.

I heard someone in the clapping circle surrounding us say our family looked so close and caring. She couldn't begin to know. We had our adversity, perhaps more than our share, but each taste of hardship had brought us closer, and made us more caring and accepting of each other.

I looked at my son, Josh, an adult of twenty-four. Yesterday he had called to say he'd be on a later flight but would still join us in plenty of time. Of course, who knew that in that one hour they'd close the airport because of weather? He ran around trying to get on any flight he could. He looked into rental cars, a bus, or a train. He had to be at his sister's wedding. He had to. He finally arrived at two a.m., only hours before the wedding. I knew he would. I knew he'd find a way.

I watched my son-in-law, my new son, Daniel. I smiled as I remembered their first and only argument. He wanted her to go with him to a friend's wedding. She was not able to take the day off work. They could not stand to be parted from each other even for one day. Something might happen...

Little did we know what waited for them just a few months away. The horror that waited for us all.

finally discovered them in jail, awaiting transport to prison.

I told him I didn't appreciate his sick humor. He ignored my comment and left me the name and phone number of the man at the U. S. Embassy who was working on the case. He promised to call back as soon as he knew anything else.

I was definitely awake now, though I wished I was dreaming. My head couldn't really absorb what had happened. I actually pinched myself, hoping against hope I wouldn't feel this additional stab of pain and know I was having a nightmare. But the pain was there. It was everywhere. I called my husband, neither of us knowing where to begin or what to do.

When we tried to get in touch with Daniel and Miriam, we were told the prison rules did not allow them contact with anyone — no phone calls, no letters. I wanted to go to France immediately. However, I was asked to wait. Seeing them would require permission from the judge. That would take time.

They had spent four days in jail and were now being sent to separate prisons to await trial. One prison was in a northern suburb and the other in the extreme south of Paris. We still had not heard from them directly, as they had not yet received permission to have contact with anyone.

4

A Volunteer Visitor

We were contacted by a volunteer from the CADI (Comite D'aide aux Detenus Israelites), a Jewish community agency seeking to identify Jews in French prisons. This incredible organization sends visitors to see prisoners and tries to help meet their physical and spiritual needs.

I will always be grateful to Edouard for his swift contact with us. News of our children was precious. His attempt at English was so heartwarming. It read:

Dear friends,

I saw again your son-in-law this morning. This afternoon the man of the American consulate came to see him and by the way I met him. The lawyer is now officially designated (from today). The 1500 francs will be put on his account tomorrow, Friday.

Your son-in-law get his tallith and tephilins. The consulate transmitted him the letters you sent by express.

The judge gave him permission to send you and to receive letters directly and not through the judge's office as usual. He asks me to say two things: He was enough happy by the fact you intended to come, he kisses you and blesses you, but he asks not to come now. And not to come before things are a little bit settled. For example: he is in jail in the north. But there, no place for the women, that was why your daughter was sent south. But in the south, near the women's prison, is the biggest men's prison of France. He has the possibility to ask to be transferred there, so that he'll have possibility to visit his wife. He put this demand when the consulate was with him. So he, and both the man of the consulate and me, we think it's be more wise to wait a bit before coming.

The second thing is to announce you that your daughter is three month expectant mother. He is sad to have to say that in such bad circumstances. They planned to give you the good news on the first of May. But I tell you personally now, that the medical service in jail is a very good one, and each prisoner is examinated within 48 hours they arrive. So don't be too much worried.

I fax your letter to CADI so that they'll have your phone number. If there is nobody to visit your daughter I'll try to manage to see her but, unfortunately, I couldn't go regularly. But keep good hope: Gott whet helfen (G-d will help)! I understand you deeply well, but don't be desperate, there is a lot of people involved in your children's case. In a few days the situation will be more settled. I am sure that your son-in-law will do all he can do to put his wife out of that nightmare as soon as possible.

Keep you in good health: this is the best thing you can do for the kids. They must have all their strength for their case.

If I could write you in French be sure I won't be so rude and tough. I stay at your disposition.

Monsieur Edouard

5
The Nightmare Begins

ooks and other media were my only reference to prison life, and I was haunted by thoughts of beatings, starvation, mistreatment, and doctors using unsterile materials for exams. Nightmares filled my waking and sleeping hours. Neither Daniel nor Miriam had phone privileges. We could not hear their voices or know firsthand if they were okay. Our only contact was through the United States Embassy or the CADI volunteers, to whom we gave messages and then waited for news.

Finally, the CADI worker called. "Are they safe?" was my first question and main concern.

Clearly insulted, he said, "We are not the United States, we are a civilized country. Of course they are safe."

I slept better that night, but not much. At least we had a caring, consistent contact, someone who had seen my son-in-law and had spoken with him. At least Daniel knew we were involved and what we had done so far.

Now how to establish that contact with my daughter? She was pregnant. I wept that night, not from joy, but terror. I had so many questions. What kind of care was she receiving? Was her food adequate to sustain the baby? How would they get kosher food? How would the emotional stress affect the baby? How in the world had this happened? What had they been charged with? What had they done or not done? This could not be happening to them...to me. This surely was a bad dream, a horrendous nightmare.

Several days later, we finally got my daughter's first letter.

To My Dear Sweet Parents:

Oh Mom and Dad, I am so sorry about this whole mess. I feel badly about the whole thing and I'm sorry to be bringing pain into the family. I love you so much and I miss you terribly.

We were trying so hard not to say anything about the baby until a full three months had passed, so we didn't tell you on Pesach. How I wish we had. To find out from some authority and not from us... I wish we could have told you ourselves. The baby and I are, baruch Hashem, fine. We feel good and we can't wait to see you again.

I wrote to friends close by, asking them to send you this letter by fax because the mail here is very slow and I am limited by my supply of stamps. Thank you for the money. It is an unbelievable necessity for us. The lawyer you hired has been really nice. I wrote a letter thanking him and asking him what the charges against us are. I also asked him about the other lawyer I hired. When I came here, I had no lawyer, so I wrote to one from a list they gave me, asking him to represent me. I haven't heard from him yet.

The baby is due November 12th, G-d willing. I had an appointment with my (New York) doctor today. I obviously didn't make it. We were going to see how things were and tell you about the baby this weekend.

The conditions here are, baruch Hashem, fine. I will be moved to the prison nursery for pregnant women, probably late next week or soon thereafter, but for now I share a room with a nice French lady who has been here for eleven months of a two-year sentence. She has been very helpful explaining things to me.

I thank G-d for giving me such wonderful, supportive, understanding, and loving parents, and for giving me my special husband. Daniel and I hope that he will be transferred to the men's division of this prison and that we will get visitation rights. It will be difficult to see him because I will know that our time will be very limited, but I miss him too much to be apart from him for so long.

France, thank G-d, has a big Jewish community. I cannot imagine how much worse the situation would be if we didn't have the support from the Jewish community.

I am eating all right, baruch Hashem. Mostly fruits, veggies, milk, bread, and a sour cream—like cheese thing. It had a hechsher on it. Now that I have money I can buy kosher food, so I will have more to eat. My roommate gives me her milk every day for the baby.

I want you to know that after reading your letter (forwarded to me) from the embassy, I feel better. I wasn't having a great day. It's very cloudy and erev Shabbos. I had a good cry from your letter, and I feel myself again. My spirits are very good. I am holding strong onto my faith in Hashem, and I am doing remarkably well (if I say so myself).

I will write again if there's anything important or after I receive a letter from you... Please write to Daniel. I, at least, have the baby keeping me company, but he is all alone.

Please send us pictures. I have one picture of you at your wedding and I look at it all the time. I also have an ultrasound picture of the baby. I had two, and I sent one to Daniel.

We were thinking of ways to tell you about the baby, and we thought of faxing you a copy of the ultrasound (the one I would've had today), writing on it, "Get the picture, Bubby and Zaidy?!" That was just one idea, though.

How is Bubby doing? I'm sorry that I'm not there for her. I know how much she needs my company and help. What, if anything, are we going to tell her? I worry she won't handle it well because of her health. Oy! There are so many tzaros in the world. We must do our best to ask Hashem for a yeshuah for everything.

Five of my friends are expecting, G-d willing, around the same time as we are. It will be so nice for all the kids to be friends with each other. It's very exciting. I look basically the same, but in a little while I will need bigger clothing, G-d willing. There is a place that you can send packages to; no food but you can send clothes and pictures and cards and stamps, etc. The jail doesn't accept any packages. They are afraid of bombs or something.

Once I meet with the lawyer, we will have a better idea of how long I'll be here. I want very much to push for the judge to allow a family in France to bail me out. If you could see what can be done in that vein I would be very grateful.

I daven to Hashem that this baby should not be born here. They send you to a regular hospital, but then you and the baby come back here. I want to be at home, but any regular place outside of prison will be fine. I think about making a Kiddush or a bris and pidyon haben in prison, and it just doesn't seem to work right.

There is a rabbi who visits the prison. I met him today. He gave me a French Jewish newspaper and told me what time Shabbos begins. Please ask a rav what I do about candle lighting. Do I light on a bulb if I have nothing else? Will I need to light an extra candle when I come home? I have a minchah/maariv siddur, and the rabbi said he will get me a Tanach next week.

Life here is not that bad. Baruch Hashem, I have much holding me up; you, my husband, the baby, Hashem. I feel closer to Hashem because of this. I feel extremely connected, more than ever before.

I love you tremendously.

Your baby girl and her baby

She had hoped this letter would reassure us, calm us. But I could hear the whisper of terror beneath the words of strength and spirituality. *Baruch Hashem*, the phrase that thanks and acknowledges G-d, punctuated every other sentence. Now it sounded more like a mantra begging G-d for help than an expression of praise.

Reuben and I had no idea of the charges or how to deal with it. A puzzle of panic overwhelmed us. Where to begin? How to begin? What to do? We were attacked by an avalanche of unknowns:

The French legal system, how does it work?

Prison, how were they living?

What were they eating? Was kosher food available to them?

Did they have money we sent? Did they need more money? How much?

Did they sleep on a bed, a slab, the floor?

Were they being beaten by the guards or by other inmates?

Could they communicate with each other or those around them? How would they make their needs known? Would their English be understood?

An endless cacophony of questions pounded me and my husband till we were spent. Everything in our daily lives disappeared, pushed out by our fears. We, too, had become prisoners. Prisoners of our emotions and thoughts.

6

Disastrous Favor

When we spoke about it many months later, I found out that the conditions in the general prison were not as good as in the nursery and she had not been "fine." Miriam, scared and hungry, was determined to live religiously and keep kosher. Yet how?

The lawyer we hired was not able to talk to her until she signed up with him. She was required to fax the Palais de Justice (the Palace of Justice) requesting him as her lawyer. But when she tried to, she was told that her authorization could not be processed because the fax machine at the Palais was out of ink. It took seven days for them to get a refill cartridge.

That was my first of many frustrations in dealing with a system that works so differently from the American one. It was also the beginning of meeting and dealing with people who went beyond what I ever would have expected. They did so much in order to help our family, who were strangers to them. I will be grateful to them for the rest of our lives.

Daniel was never transferred from his prison. The prison Miriam was in was tougher, with lots of problems and overcrowded conditions. It was a tinderbox that frequently exploded and was considered much more dangerous than Daniel's. We were told that even if he was transferred and they were in the same prison, they probably would not be able to see each other until after the trial. That could take years.

Surely things couldn't get worse.

My mother, eighty-nine, kept calling to inquire about their extended absence. She missed their frequent visits and phone calls. Eventually we had to tell her the truth.

Miriam and Daniel had boarded a plane in France eager to return home after a wonderful few days' vacation. They had checked the suitcase Daniel's good friend had asked them to take home for him along with their own luggage. The friend had begged this favor of them in order to get back his suitcase and its contents. At least that's what he had said.

When they were already sitting in their seats, a stewardess announced a slight delay, due to a customs problem. Two officers boarded the plane and went directly to them. After checking their identification, they were asked to accompany these officers and were taken off the plane.

"Why?" they asked. "Is there a problem?"

"No, nothing wrong," they were told. "This is just routine. Don't be concerned, the plane can wait for you."

Frightened, they were escorted through the airport to a small room in the basement. On one side of the room was their luggage. In the center of the room, on a table, was the suitcase they had been asked to take by Daniel's friend, his best friend's brother, whom he had known for years.

"Is this suitcase yours?"

"No," they replied. They explained who had given them the suitcase and the circumstances around it.

"Why didn't you say that it wasn't yours when you checked in?"

"No one asked."

"Open it!"

Fear turned into panic. Without the key, Daniel struggled for several minutes until he was able to break open the suitcase. Inside, they found socks: many, many, many socks. The suitcase seemed filled with socks.

My children looked at each other, puzzled. Terror began to replace panic.

At this point, they were separated. My daughter was taken to an adjoining room and handcuffed to a bench. My son-in-law remained with the suitcase. They were ordered not to speak to each other.

Daniel watched as a sock was taken from the suitcase and opened. Inside was a Ziploc bag full of pills with cartoon characters printed on them. His mind began to race.

"What is this?" he was asked.

"Children's vitamins?" Half joking, his mind a blank, Daniel could not comprehend what was really there.

The customs officers opened sock after sock. More and more pills rolled out. As they opened each sock, Daniel yelled to my daughter, "It's pills. Oh G-d, there's more!"

Stunned by the contents of the suitcase, they slowly began to realize the severity of the situation.

"The police have been called."

Instead of fear, Daniel and Miriam were relieved. They would now be able to tell their story. They would tell the police who gave them the suitcase and to whom they had been asked to bring it. Everything, they now thought, would be straightened out. The police would capture the true culprits and they would go home.

They had no idea how unrealistic their thinking was. They were in the possession of drugs. That was it. The police had no interest in their story.

This all took place over twenty years ago, when the world was a different place, and the events of 9/11 had not yet occurred. Travelers were rarely asked questions at check-in; rarely asked if they had packed their own suitcase or if they were taking a package for someone. People were more trusting and routinely took parcels for strangers, trusting good friends when asked, like Daniel and Miriam had. Our religious community was even more naive and was eager to help another. It was a mitzvah, after all.

And that was how Miriam and Daniel found themselves taken to a jail and placed in separate cells. They could speak to each other only if they yelled loudly enough, but they could not see each other. Their cells were bare. For four days they slept on slabs coming out of the wall and subsisted on fruit and vegetables.

After four days of questioning, each was sent before a judge. Miriam's glasses had been confiscated. She could not make out the face of the judge. Was Her Honor sympathetic or scornful? Did she believe her at all?

With all these questions unanswered, Miriam and Daniel were taken from their cells. Only their yelled good-byes could be heard as they were driven off to different prisons at opposite ends of the city.

7
A Plea for Help

This letter was sent to the family my daughter lived with when she was away at school. They had become her second family and shared a unique bond. In fact, it was Aaron who had gone to the airport to pick them up and found they were missing. It was Aaron who called me that eventful Wednesday morning to tell us what was happening.

Dear Aaron and Rachel and my favorite kids,

Well, here is the situation. I am in a French prison. I don't think I can say anymore right now, but with much help from Hashem, I will tell you in person soon. All I can say is that this is a dire situation, and we need all the help we can get. I don't know who, but someone, maybe my parents or maybe you guys, sent Lubavitch to us with food. Baruch Hashem, that was very helpful. But now the prison I am in doesn't allow any outside food. It is very hard to find fruit here. I am only here one day, and baruch Hashem I am managing.

Here is the kicker. Daniel and I are expecting! I am just three months this week. I have a lawyer here. I will be meeting him soon. He is supposedly good, but he will cost money, of which I have none. We had $600 cash that was confiscated and credit cards are not accepted. So please send a copy of this letter to my parents and just tell them what's up. Tell them they can skip the video camera as a baby gift and I'll take their help now instead.

I don't know what's going on with our bills and apartment. If you can find out how to take care of these things, please do. I appreciate your help so much. I miss you guys and I can't wait to see you.

I don't know if or at what price the bail will be. We are working on bailing me out to a family in France. If they set a price I'm sure it will be high. Please tell my parents that there are doctors here who check on our health and I am feeling fine, baruch Hashem. I am writing to you because I hope the letter will get to you sooner because you live closer. Tell my parents I love them, and with much help from Hashem we will be together soon.

If you can, send clothing (sweat suit, undershirts, and elastic-waist skirts). No navy-blue colored clothes are allowed. Maybe a windbreaker, too. Thank you! Also, send pictures to me, too, please or whatever you can — not food — they don't allow outside food.

I don't know my husband's prison number or his cell number. I told him to write to you also if he can. I have not been in touch with him since Monday when we went to separate prisons.

Thank you so much for your help. Please give kisses to the kids.

This letter and the one to us had been sent at the same time. Miriam was desperately trying to reach us for help. Even if that help came only one day sooner, it would have meant the world to her.

The lawyer she selected was not the one we had engaged. It took weeks to straighten it out. At their wedding, I had promised a video camera as a first baby gift, so that we and our grandchild could keep in touch. She was offering to trade the camera in for help now. How bizarre for her to think she needed to barter for our help. It only heightened my realization that fear had made her irrational.

The letters sounded so positive and so strong. But mothers know their children and I could hear the fear and terror hiding under the words and the confusion and denial of her situation as she rambled from topic to topic.

Monday

Dear Mom, Dad, and Josh:

The rabbi came today and brought me your letter and a huge bag of kosher food. Hashem is very busy at His wonders. In this prison they offer kosher food for sale every other week and you receive it the following week, which means my food supply would've been very limited had the rabbi not brought me food.

Your prayers are working. We must be patient, though; the French system is different than in America. And Hashem has a plan to be carried out. Be comforted to know that your grandchild to be and I are doing well. There are improvements each day.

How are Mom's eyes? And back? And sleep! You grandparents-to-be must get your rest. Leave things to Hashem. He's had experience with running the world and is taking care of the three of us! You can daven to Hashem to let Him know your feelings but you must also take care of yourself. Baruch Hashem, I am doing fine over here. I've written to the judge to get the lawyer changed to the one you hired.

Tuesday

A social worker came to see me today to tell me to write to the old lawyer to cancel him, and again to the judge requesting the new lawyer. The woman told me my new lawyer plans to see the judge on Thursday! So things may start moving.

I'm sure a lot is going on, but over here I know nothing. I have good spirits. The little neshamaleh and I are holding on tight to our faith and trust in Hashem. He has proven to be looking out for us. And Daniel tells me (although he also gets bored and frustrated at times) he is in a good place, not physically (well, it's clean and decent), but, well, you know what I mean. His head. We are more connected to Hashem now than ever.

How is Bubby? What will we tell her? She is sure to notice my absence soon, if she hasn't already. I was planning a visit to you this summer, but whenever I get out of here I think will be a perfect time to visit you guys. I miss you more than ever.

So Josh, can you believe this? Are you ready to be an uncle? Don't worry, I'll give you until November (G-d willing). I've received a few letters from you through the embassy and the rabbi. Thank you for your support and encouragement.

Don't make a trip to France. It may not be necessary, and it's very complicated to get a visit with either of us anyway. Perhaps we'll hear from the lawyer tomorrow and have an idea of the judge's plans for us. Daven good and strong for us. It's all that we can do and the best we can do. I'll leave room to write more tomorrow. I love you very much.

Thursday

Well, I just met with your lawyer and his colleague. They are both so very nice. They tell me you are coming next Wednesday for three weeks. I hope you have all the visiting permissions set up. You should also do some touring. France is beautiful. The weather is strange — 55° sometimes, but it often gets cloudy and rains. It's chilly, too.

I'm very comforted by meeting the lawyers today. I see that the waiting won't be forever and things are moving. I have such a great feeling from all that the lawyers told me and what our friend Aaron is doing and has done.

It makes me feel so good to know that I have family (friends included)

I can count on. Aaron is wonderful, baruch Hashem. Yes, maybe a malach, but more likely a hidden tzaddik.

Well, I'll leave some more space to write tomorrow. When you come, G-d willing, we may be close to arranging a release for me to a French family. Please bring pictures of the family and of my wedding. There isn't much they allow you to bring, just clothes and books. Maybe bring a Tanach for Daniel. He has a Kitzur and, I think, his siddur and tallis and tefillin. Some pictures would be a nice comfort. Oh, and a pair of slippers. I'll write more tomorrow. Much love from me and the little neshamaleh (who is still very quiet).

It's Friday, almost lunchtime. I expect to see the rabbi soon. So I'll finish this letter now and make sure it's ready for the mail. Oh, tell the lawyer that I heard from the nun here that visits between prisoners are usually not allowed until after they've both been judged. So even if we had Daniel transferred here (to a bigger, not as good prison), we wouldn't be able to see each other. So he should focus on getting us out on bail.

Well, I love you guys tons and hope you have a nice Shabbos! (It's our ten-month anniversary.)

Love, ♡
Your baby Miriam and her baby

The letters began to come regularly, but the mail from France was slow. The information in her letters would tell us of events from two weeks before, so the news was overlapping and stale. Her letters reminded me of a volcano, with its visual beauty on top and hot molten lava underneath. I wondered when the volcano would erupt, destroying whatever was in its path.

I had recently undergone three surgeries on my right eye, and my vision was weak. Her concern and questions about my eyes and our general health and her grandmother was humbling. I hoped focusing on us gave her some respite from her own dire situation.

The food situation worried me. What was she eating when she

couldn't get kosher food? Was her lack of nourishment putting herself and her baby in danger? Her adding a bit of news each day made me wonder if there was a need to conserve paper.

We were to learn later that everything, from writing paper, pens, and stamps to soap detergent, hand soap, and toilet paper, could be bought but were not supplied automatically. Prisoners needed a constant supply of money to buy food and the basics we take for granted. I was getting hints at a life that was so alien to ours. A life that was now my daughter's daily routine.

8

Support Has No Borders

*O*ur synagogue rabbi received this letter from our daughter. He was amazed at her selflessness and concern for us. Meanwhile, I was arranging my trip to France.

My husband, Reuben, had suffered from multiple sclerosis for almost fifteen years and was confined to a wheelchair. There was no way he could accompany me. Planning this trip would also have to involve arranging support for him at home.

I could not speak French. I knew no one in France, had no idea where I would stay, or how I would navigate the French prison system. I was scared to make the trip, but more frightened not to.

Tuesday, 25 Iyar
40 days in the Omer

Dear Rabbi Berger, amush,

I'm not sure where to begin this letter. I don't know what you are already aware of, and I'd like to keep this brief. My husband and I are in separate prisons in France. We have our physical needs met and our spiritual ones are being helped by the rabbis in the prisons and by Chabad.

Baruch Hashem, we are both using this time very constructively. We have seen it as a gift from Hashem. A chance to devote time, all our time, to personal growth. As you may know, we are expecting, b'sha'ah tovah. We feel that Hashem has given us a timeout from our mundane lives to devote to our neshamos, before our lives get more complicated and devoting time to ourselves becomes even more difficult.

I am afraid, however, that my family is suffering greatly from this. I feel they have many strong fears that are blinding them from the incredible positive side of this. I will see my mother and brother soon and assure them that we are all doing well. But my father is unable to visit and get this personal assurance. I feel he has many moments of overwhelming grief.

I ask that you help my father and my family through this. This is a request for you to encourage them to be positive. See how they are doing each day. Do not let them feel alone in this. Please, reach out to them. They are hurting. I would be forever grateful to you for helping sustain my family through this crisis.

I have a second request. I would like to ask the Rebbe for a berachah. I do not know how. If it is possible, could you request, on my family's behalf, a berachah for a yeshuah from imprisonment?

When I decided to ask for a berachah, I realized there are many things I would like to ask the Rebbe for help with. I will tell them to you, and, if it is appropriate, perhaps you can pass them along to the Rebbe.

The first is a complete refuah for my father. I know that would require a great nes, but it's one of my greatest wishes.

The second is a berachah that my husband and I should have many healthy children who are ovdei Hashem.

The last is that we be released as soon as possible, together, so we *can be a family again and build a bayis ne'eman b'Yisrael.*

These requests are not in order of importance. They are all equally important to me.

Thank you for your time and consideration. Thank you for your help. May we merit the speedy coming of Mashiach.

Miriam

When the rabbi received the letter from our daughter, he called and shared it with us. He had only recently found out of Daniel and Miriam's imprisonment — we had tried desperately to keep it under wraps both because we knew so little and because we craved privacy. The Rebbe Miriam referred to was the Lubavitcher Rebbe, who was still alive at the time.

The rabbi had received a call from a woman in New York who told him she was desperate for our phone number. She wanted to "help." She told him as much as she knew of the story while all the while trying to glean as much new information as she could from him.

We begged his confidence and told him how this same woman — a complete stranger — not only had our number but had called us the day before. She had tried to get information from me, and when I refused, she screamed at me. She questioned what kind of mother I was because I had not yet flown to France. She demanded I go immediately — and hire her cousin as my driver, for $300 a day.

I don't know, or care, whether she was motivated by a search for information and gossip or a desire to get her French cousin work. At any event, we asked our rabbi to refer all calls to us and give people no information. Dealing with the situation was difficult enough. "Helpers" made it that much harder.

When the rabbi faxed us a copy of my daughter's letter, I couldn't help but compare the two attitudes: caring versus callous. My daughter's letter of concern for us and the gossiping stranger motivated by her own needs.

9
A Dreaded Trip

Dear Mom and Dad,

The lawyer tells me Mom and Josh are coming for three weeks. If this letter gets to you before you leave, please bring some things for us. T-shirt-style undershirts and a pair of shorts for Daniel, and two or three cotton button-down shirts for the summer and an elastic-waist skirt for me. And a watch or clock.

The weather has quickly improved. It's about 80° each day and usually sunny till 7 or 8:00! Days are very long here. Also maybe p.j.'s for us. For me, a T-shirt is fine. Thank you for this and for all the support you are giving us. Oh, a sheitel clip, like one of the ones I bought you. Your care and love for us has been lifesaving.

Baruch Hashem, we have family and friends who care so much for us. We are doing well — all "three" of us. We both have plenty of food, paper, envelopes (and soon stamps). We are, baruch Hashem, in a very positive mind space. We are using this as an opportunity to grow.

I came to a realization on Shabbos. We know that Hashem is in charge and has a plan. We know He only does good. So this is part of His plan and is good.

Of course, it's hard to sit patiently and wait till we see it. But in part we don't have to. Already we have seen that this is a fantastic opportunity for us as soon-to-be parents. Most people realize that their life is in need of refreshing, of fixing, only too late, once they have already passed their errors on to their children. Hashem has given us a berachah that we should open our eyes and see what in our life needs revamping. What can we fix? What can we do better for our neshamos, for each other, for our children? Before they are here and we are too busy to notice that which is missing.

This opportunity to be alone, physically, with nothing to do but think and introspect. Why did this happen to me? Not in a depressed, do-nothing way. But in an active way. This must mean something for me. Let me see what it is and get to fixing it, so I can get home and put into place our new demands for ourselves.

This must also have a meaning for you as our family. You and we and everyone that this affects should take it personally.

We were put in prison in France. Taken away from you — not in New York or Miami — but in France, where everything is foreign. We are very far away — why? Each of us has something in our lives that needs improvement. I will do my part. Baruch Hashem, Daniel and I have this chance to fix our lives before we are given another life, G-d willing, to affect. Before Hashem gives us the children whose lives we will guide and mold, we as parents need to be at our best so we can give our best to our children. So that's our part, to improve our neshamos to be able to be the best parents (and children) that we can, before "life" gets in the way. We are happily busy doing that and we are connected to Hashem and to our emunah.

Please do not worry too much about us. Everything has its time. A bris at eight days and pregnancy at nine months. This, too, has its time and can't last one day less or one day more. We don't have the comfort to know the length of time, but that is where our bitachon and emunah come in. Hashem knows the time and knows what we need. He provides for us. Trust Him.

Anyway, enough for today. I have another sonogram scheduled for Tuesday. I'll let you know how your grandchild is doing. Till then — hold on tight! We love you.

Tuesday

The baby has grown healthily, baruch Hashem. I could see the face, a nose, and jaw and it was moving all over. Wow! This is such a miracle, such a blessing from Hashem. I only wish I could share it more with Daniel and you. Soon, im yirtzeh Hashem.

I didn't receive any letters from the lawyer or you today so I don't know when your visit is. Well, much love.

Thursday

I got two cards today — thank you so much. And three letters with pictures. Please send more pix. Yes, I would love to see you too, Dad. Please try to keep as positive as you can. I assure you that we (the "three" of us) are all doing wonderfully. It'd only be better if we were at home. We have all the necessities and support and love from you. We are, as always, in the hands of Hashem, who carries us through this. Try, I know it's hard. I, too, cry sometimes and feel very frustrated and useless. But those negative thoughts — we must push them out and fill our mind with positives.

Daddy, we are fine and getting better each day. Please try to accept that. G-d willing, as soon as we are out of France I will come and spend some time at home with our family. In the meantime, you have my love and I live in your heart, so we are together. At night, all our neshamos go to Hashem and spend time together. So make sure you sleep.

I dreaded going to France alone. My son Josh took a month off work to accompany me. It was a G-dsend. I would not have managed without his strength, support, and humor. We became closer in the process, while we supported each other, his sister, and his brother-in-law.

At that time, the airfare was exorbitant. To reduce the price of our tickets by half, we booked a flight that flew to Minneapolis, then to Amsterdam, and finally, after a ten-hour wait, on to France.

Instead of waiting, depressed, in the Amsterdam airport for all those hours, my son insisted that we pass the time by exploring the city. Exiting the airport, I passed customs first and sat on a bench to wait for him. Josh was disappointed that they hadn't stamped his passport indicating he had indeed been to Amsterdam. I had to laugh as I watched him re-enter the customs area and exit it repeatedly until his passport received his prized stamp, "Amsterdam." Perhaps my laughter was his intention.

I followed him passively to the local train, on which we traveled into the heart of the city. After wandering through the Anne Frank House and another museum with happy tourists, my depression and anxiety began to get the better of me. Taking the lead, Josh took me to The Grasshopper, a famous local establishment, for coffee.

We had rented a small bachelor apartment in the Latin Quarter of Paris. It had a tiny kitchenette and came equipped with everything we needed: washer, dryer, and answering machine. There was a sofa bed for me in the one main room, and we found that if we carefully let some air out of the blowup mattress my son used as a bed, it fit from wall to wall on the entire floor of the tiny kitchen. Then he could close the kitchen door and have his own room (providing, of course, that he didn't stand or move too much). It was a six-story walkup, so we planned our trips carefully.

10
Navigating All Things Foreign

We got up early on our first morning in Paris and walked down our six flights. We had pored over maps the night before, figuring out how to get where we needed to go by the local Metro. We bought a five-day Metro pass for 120 francs, only to discover later that a seven-day pass, covering a smaller area, would have been only 80 francs and would have met our needs just as well.

We needed identity pictures for our passes. The Metro station near our apartment had a photo machine just waiting for us. Of course, the instructions were in French, of which we spoke and read not a word. My son, assuring me he knew what to do, sat down in the booth, put in the 20 francs and pressed the appropriate buttons.

Two four-by-six mug shots emerged. We decided this was not quite right for the two-inch square provided for the identity photo on our Metro pass cards. He tried again, and twenty tiny half-inch pictures emerged. Wrong again! As there was only one choice left, we finally hit pay dirt. Our picture adventure was the only smile we had that day.

After getting lost several times and having every Frenchman we asked directions of either ignore us or give us a hand motion I had never seen before, we finally made it to the Embassy. The line of French citizens waiting to apply for visas went around the block. All we needed to do was flash our passports and we were escorted, by a heavily armed soldier, to the front of the line and into the embassy. It was a strange yet secure feeling being on home soil in the middle of a foreign country. I hoped that positive feeling would stay with us and be a sign of good things to come.

Our contact at the embassy was the Citizen Service Officer. He was a wonderful, caring gentleman who had already met with our lawyers. He gave us directions to the Palais de Justice and had a letter ready for us to take. The letter, in French, explained who we were, who our children were, the charges of drug trafficking against them, the judge's name, and that we wanted permission from the judge to visit them in their prisons. We had been told to bring passport pictures with us. We would need these pictures for our prison visitor identity cards, if indeed the judge would allow us to visit. And so we were prepared — or so I thought.

We exited the Metro with no idea of where to go. It is very difficult to get directions to a place you can barely pronounce when you don't know French and people refuse to speak English, even when they can. A dismissive wave of both hands from the shoulders into the air was a response with which we became very familiar. But all this frustration was just a prelude. When we finally reached the Palais de Justice, the torture really began.

I repeatedly showed the letter we had been given to anyone who looked like they could help us find the office we needed. I was embarrassed by its contents and I had to resist an incredibly strong desire to tell everyone who read it that my children really hadn't done anything wrong.

When reader after reader seemed to show no reaction to the fact that I was a mother of "drug traffickers," it began to dawn on me that anyone having business in this building was either a criminal, a lawyer, or a close relative or friend of the accused, and I had better get used to my new community of peers.

But now, being part of this community, people did try to help us find our way. We did not understand their responses. The sign language they thought would help us got us lost several times. Each time we'd go back to the entrance of the building and start again, ask for help, show the letter, and get directions. The pain, shame, frustration, confusion, and desperation was overwhelming. I wanted to yell at everyone we passed and beg them for help, but I knew it would do no good.

It took two frustrating hours until we found our way to the right department. We handed in our pictures, passports, and letter of request and were told to wait. And wait we did. After almost another two hours, we were called to the window and told by the clerk that our request would be processed. It would take about a week until we could get permission to see Miriam and Daniel, if indeed the judge would grant it. We had no guarantee that she would.

We exited the Palais de Justice almost five hours after we had entered. The stress and tension of the past several weeks, the jet lag, and the frustration of the day engulfed me. I felt weak and in pain.

I looked around for a bench so I could rest for a few minutes. There were none in sight. I sat down on the concrete sidewalk and cried for the first time since I had heard the horrible news.

11
Parlez-vous Anglais?

We waited and waited to hear if our request for visiting permits would be approved by the judge. I never realized how loud — even deafening — silence is when you are waiting for a phone that does not ring and a fax that does not come. Not knowing the judge's decision filled every inch of our being with stress. I would not, could not, believe we had come all this way just to be refused visitation.

After two days of sitting in our cramped quarters, waiting for the phone to ring, my son insisted we walk around and "do something." Our apartment was so small he predicted that if we just waited in our room for "the call," one of us would eventually throw the other out of the sixth-story window. Our only window.

I followed him around France, grateful for his support. I thanked G-d for my adult children, who knew when it was appropriate to care for their parents and when to let themselves be cared for.

One afternoon, having no desire to go outside and sightsee yet again, I convinced my son to let me stay in our apartment as he went off to explore Paris on rollerblades.

Stopping for a drink at a cafe, he was approached by an elderly couple, who hesitantly asked, *"Parlez-vous Anglais?"*

Obviously relieved and clearly delighted at having found someone who would help them in English, this couple from the Midwestern United States told Josh they were lost. They had not been able to find anyone who would help them. Josh took out his map and began to give them instructions. Seeing their confusion and armed with his experience of the last few days, he decided to take them to the Central Station instead. Once there, sensing their insecurity, he accompanied them on the train all the way to their suburban destination.

Back on familiar ground, the relieved couple could not stop thanking him. He refused the money they offered and wished them a pleasant vacation. "You tell your parents what a wonderful son they have," instructed the woman. But of course, I already knew that.

The days dragged on.

After five days of waiting, the phone call finally came. The judge would allow us visitation.

The first week of appointments had already been scheduled. When I heard of the timetable, I could not believe the cruel twist of fate. The first appointment to see my daughter was scheduled for Shabbos. I had waited weeks to see her. Weeks full of dread, anticipation, and fear, and now I could not go! I begged them to change the appointment to a weekday, but they refused. Visiting days in the women's prison were Monday, Wednesday, and Saturday only, and were scheduled one week at a time. Unless special permission for a one-hour visit was obtained, the visits would last only a half hour. This extended visit had to be requested by the prisoner and there had to be exceptional circumstances.

I panicked. Had someone told my daughter to request the longer appointments? Would they be granted? Was having traveled halfway around the world considered exceptional circumstances? All I could think about was that I was losing a precious visit with my child, my very first visit with her.

12
Haunting Sights and Sounds

I had never been to a prison before.

We got up at five a.m. the morning of our visit, which had been rescheduled for a weekday. We packed bottled water (selling for $5 US at the station) and toilet paper (not always present, especially in the prison's visitor bathrooms) and wet towelettes in ziplock bags (for hand washing, which my son said we'd want to do often, based on his experience of rollerblading around Paris). We took the local Metro to the RER (long-distance train) and from that train a bus that went to the prison.

I had to force myself to take each step. The closer we got to the prison, the harder it became. With each step a voice in my head screamed, *No! This is not happening to me, I can't do this! Let me wake up!* I was hurt and embarrassed, and a gamut of conflicting emotions fought within me. I wanted to see my daughter, to hold her, to reassure her, and I wanted to flee, go home, and hide under the covers until it was over.

It took us over three hours to reach the prison. The prison complex was the bus's last stop. With *Maison d'Arret* (prison) plastered on its windows, we knew we were on the right bus, but asked anyway. I boarded the bus, my head down, not daring to glance at other people. After a few minutes, my eyes wandered around the bus. Who else was going to the last stop? Was it that woman with the package? What was she bringing? What could we bring? So many questions.

The bus entered the prison compound. The first stop was the youth facility, the second and last stop, the men's prison. We had to get off there and were directed to a long road that ended at the women's facility.

As we followed the road, a building came into view. It looked like any other building. I couldn't see the barbed wire or guard towers or even armed guards that had been so prominent at the other two prisons. I was to discover that all the signs of a prison were there, just not from our vantage point.

People were gathered outside. It was cold, cloudy, and windy. Unsure of what to do, unsure even if we were in the right place, we approached the guard. They dismissed us with "No English." We waited, shivering in the cold, as more people gathered outside the building. As I looked around, I saw parents, relatives, friends, even children of criminals. I would have expected them to look different, set apart somehow, but I found that most of them looked just like us — they were just people with pain in their eyes.

They all seemed to know the routine, and I noticed a sense of community among them. Some greeted each other. There was one stark difference between these people and those whom we had met in the streets outside the prison complex. Here, everyone did their best to help and direct us, with pidgin English or by using sign language.

The guards said something and a line began to form by the door. A lady indicated with her hands that we should join the line. We would be let in one at a time.

The door buzzed. The first person entered. She closed the door behind her. What was inside? The next visitor was eventually buzzed in, and the door was slammed behind him by the guard.

Soon it was our turn, but Josh and I could not enter together. I went in first. The door slammed behind me. After passing through a metal detector, I followed the others and lined up at a booth. People were giving a name. Was it theirs or the prisoner's? They exchanged their identity papers for a card.

I took my passport and handed it to the guard. She smiled. With her smile, I felt the tension in my back ease just a bit. She took our passports and in exchange gave us the cards we had filled out at the Palais de Justice. It is a terrifying feeling to have your passport taken away from you in a foreign country — in a prison, no less. Somehow it makes you more vulnerable.

We continued following the line. Some people were lining up at a table, while others were going to lockers. Again, through motions and broken English, the community of visitors — people who, a month earlier, I might have shunned — showed us how to use the lockers, which needed exact change. We were allowed to take nothing with us except the card we had been given.

The table, we discovered, was for examining the things you could bring to the prisoners. Some things were allowed, some were not. *Interdit* (not allowed) was the second French term I learned. *Maison d'Arret* (prison) was the first. What a way to learn a foreign language. The prenatal vitamins I had brought were "*interdit*."

After putting the vitamins in my locker, we went upstairs, passing through yet another metal detector. There, a female guard took our card and gave us a number in exchange. For what? I wasn't sure and no one could tell me in English. We sat in a large room for what seemed like an eternity with the other visitors. Most people were quiet now, even subdued.

We waited. For what? Would my daughter be brought here? Was this how we'd visit? Finally we heard the keys jangling and the sound of a lock being opened. People quickly got up and hurriedly started going through the door. They trotted down the corridors, checking their numbers as they went.

I realized the number we had been given was the number of the visiting room. We found our room and went in. It was a small room, about six feet by six feet, with a twelve-inch table in the middle. There were three chairs, much like plastic lawn chairs, stacked on our side and a stool nailed in place on the other side.

The door was banged shut and we were locked inside. I sat locked in this room, wondering what would happen next. As we waited, the guards came again and again checking the locks, trying the doors, making sure no visitor could get out.

Finally, there was activity on the other side. Guards began unlocking the doors in the opposite wall. The women prisoners began jogging by, looking for the rooms they had been assigned.

The door opposite us opened. My daughter came in. My heart stopped.

My baby, my child, little more than a child herself. My spirits soared with joy. I hugged her till she gasped for breath, but I could not let go. I knew a guard would soon separate us. I would leave. She would not have that choice.

My daughter and I had one hour together by special permission. One precious hour where hugs said more than words. After all these weeks, only one hour — but at least we had one hour. Then, as expected, the guards came in and took her away.

Everyone else had a half hour and was forced to leave their visiting rooms while we were allowed to stay. My heart ached for these people, who had just spent more time waiting to see their loved ones than the time spent together with them. These people who had been kind enough to help and guide us through the process. We were one of them now. Full-fledged members of this, our new community.

My daughter's exit was immediately followed by the sounds of keys turning in locks and slamming doors. Guards walked by constantly, looking in and rattling the doors, making sure they were locked for the fifth and sixth time.

To this day the noise of the prison haunts me – the slam of the metal lockers, the bang of the entrance door, the jangle of keys, and the click of locks all against the drone of a language I could not understand. Even today, when I am alone and hear these sounds, my heart feels that icy hand squeezing harder and harder.

I called my husband that night and told him all the details of my visit with our daughter. How she looked. How she felt. What she was eating. I could hear his acceptance of my words, but understood how it gave him little solace. I felt like he would have no relief until he saw her for himself, which he might never be able to do.

13
Visiting Daniel

*T*he visit to Daniel, later that day, was much the same and yet very different. We traveled by bus to a different long-distance train that took us past where we had started that day and all the way to a suburb at the other end of the city. Once there, we waited for a local bus to take us to its last stop, the *Maison d'Arret*.

As the bus descended the hill just behind the prison, I was tortured by a view I had been spared when going to my daughter. I could clearly see the barbed wire that surrounded the prison. I saw the guards in their towers, their guns, the exercise yard, and bags of food hanging out of the cell windows. There was no hiding from the reality of the situation. It was laid out in front of me, real — hard and cold as the concrete wall that surrounded the prison.

The guards were, as at the women's prison, diverse — some helpful and kind, most uncaring and cold. The procedure was somewhat the same, but the physical plant quite different. Having thought we now knew what to do from our previous experience, we discovered that here things did not take place in the same order. We began, once again to ask the guards for help and direction. We received it from the visitors.

Unlike at the women's prison, we were always kept together and transported as a group. I stared, unbelieving, at the joking between the visitors. One man continued to set off the metal detector even though he had already taken off his necklace, watch, and jacket. Though I didn't understand what was said, I could surmise from the laughter of the group as he was asked to remove his belt.

I wondered how they could laugh. How could they act as if all this was normal? I wanted to run, to be anywhere but there. I kept my eyes downcast, pain clearly visible on my face.

Six months and countless trips to the prisons later, I was walking through the same metal detector, having set it off again and again, though my necklace, watch, bracelet, and jacket had all been removed one at a time. As I continued to set off the machine, a woman in our visiting group suggested, through motions, that perhaps I had clips in my hair under my hat. We all laughed as I reached up and extracted three bobby pins and walked through a silent detector.

As I was picking up my belongings, chuckling with the others in my group, I happened to see a couple standing in the corner of the very small room, waiting their turn at the metal detector. Their eyes were downcast, and pain, so much pain, was clearly written on their faces. They saw nothing funny in where they were or what had just transpired. Their expressions reflected confusion at how the rest of us could act as if this was normal. I watched them and realized that this had been me six months earlier. I marveled at what man can adjust to and how I had become a full-fledged member of this visitors' community. I knew, without a doubt, that they would soon join us.

14

The Future Isn't What We Foresaw

T his headline was clipped to the top of Miriam's next letter.
One word was underlined.

The Future Isn't What <u>We</u> Foresaw

How fitting, eh?

To my dearest Daddy bear,

I saw Mom and Josh yesterday. I will see Mom again tomorrow. I hope she has assured you of our safety. I have begun to think that perhaps we are in the safest place for the moment. I will write as often as possible just so you have a little cheery letter from your baby and her baby.

Thank you for the pictures (an interesting variety!) and all your letters.

They are wonderful to read and great to look at. Mom has more pictures for me and I just figured out how she can give them to me so I should get them soon.

We are all agreed on coming home after this is done. There I will, with G-d's help, have your grandchild and stay a while. So we'll be home for a while and you can see us often and spend time with all the "babies." G-d willing, we will come as a family to you very soon, to be with our family. I assure you we are doing well, physically, emotionally, and spiritually. This is a big eye-opener for us. Perhaps for others as well.

Please keep a smile with you always, if not on your face, then in your heart. Hashem is good and we will be together soon.

All our love,
Miriam and the neshamaleh

Fear. This was what jumped out at me as I read Miriam's letter. They had had no experience with drugs. They weren't streetwise. But if a good friend can put you in danger, make you a drug carrier without your knowledge and by doing so involve you in a crime syndicate, then you aren't safe anywhere. Everyone becomes a suspect, whether friend or strangers.

Fear is all around you. Fear of being in jail, fear of being out of jail, fear of your visitors and what you say to them. Fear of retaliation for what you have said and whom you have turned in to the police even though the police weren't interested. You fear incarceration. Even more, you fear freedom in a foreign country because you are sure of no one.

And so, Miriam felt safest in prison.

Baby. We had always joked that as my youngest child, she would always be my "baby." She had accepted it in good humor. But now she was constantly referring to herself as "baby." It screamed her needs and accentuated her fears. But we were so impotent in what we could do to help.

She had asked me to bring family photos and I had. But they had not allowed me to give them to her when I visited — *interdit*. Yet the photos my husband had sent with his letter were allowed. All mail was opened and examined before being given to the prisoners. Were photos sent through the mail allowed but hand-delivered ones forbidden?

There was a mailbox outside the prison. Taking a chance, I addressed the photos to her and placed them in the box. A few days later, Miriam received them.

15
Daily Miracles

My Dearest Daddy,

Well, I mailed a letter to you on Tuesday and I know you're talking to Mom here each day so this will be a short letter, but it's filled with TONS of love from both of us.

I saw the lawyers on Wednesday. Mom saw them today. I'm sure she told you what they said. They're working on getting us both released to families in France. They have jobs waiting (at least for me — I don't know about my hubby). They hope that I'll be released, but it's harder to get Daniel out. My file is more innocent because it seems they see me only as an accomplice because I never handled the bags, etc.

Anyway, I'm sure Mom will tell you all that. I just want to let you know that I'm doing really well. Today was actually a great day, despite the fact that it's some national holiday and there's no mail or canteen delivery (things that are highlights of the day). But I have strong faith and I really had a super day, thank G-d.

I hope you have many good days also. I know it's hard. Things are so unknown, which causes doubts, fears, worries, all that grows into crazy nightmares — but only if we let them. We must focus on the positives. Oh, ask Mom about the food I got on Wednesday! It's just one of many miracles that are going on now in our lives — just open your eyes and you'll also see them.

Well, I hope you have a good Shabbos. You're at my table as I am at yours. We're anxiously awaiting our release and our opportunity to come home and be with you. Oh, start getting used to the sound of "Zaidy." Mom was confused when I introduced her to the baby as "Bubby."

Lots of love, hugs, and kisses,
The babies ☺ ♡

P.S. Thanks for all your letters. Have a great yom tov. Learn lots of Torah! Your graphics are great! I'll see Mom and Josh today, so I'll send more love through them!

We met with the lawyers to go over the situation. The French system is so very different from the legal system in the States. The French apply Napoleonic Law, one aspect of which is that the defendant is de facto considered guilty until proven innocent.

The first judge Daniel and Miriam would see was there to give an objective opinion and to determine if a bail-like program was appropriate. Her findings and recommendations would then go before a tribunal of judges and a prosecutor, and they would determine Daniel and Miriam's fate. (This process could take between two and three years.) The maximum sentences could be as long as ten years. Since a prisoner had already served a few years before trial, the trial was usually the end product. It would take the first judge anywhere from a few weeks to a few months to review the case. So it was slowly becoming clear that Daniel and Miriam would not be returning home with me.

My kids had inadvertently and innocently walked into the middle of an international drug ring. There was speculation that they had been set up to be caught so that other carriers, on the same flight, would be able to bring in their drugs in smaller amounts. Regardless, France was cracking down on drug carriers, or mules, as they are known. The difficulty was getting anyone to believe they didn't know they were carrying drugs. No one is thought to still be that naive. But they were.

We hoped that they would be released to a French family. They would then have freedom in France, though they would be unable to leave the country and would have to frequently report to the police station. There was more hope of this outcome for Miriam, who had never gotten around to changing her maiden name on her passport after marriage, so their tickets were issued under different names. The suitcase had been picked up and checked in by Daniel under his name alone.

The lawyers were trying to put together sponsors just in case the judge would allow bail. Employment was a precondition to bail, and the Hebrew school agreed to allow Miriam to be a teacher's assistant if she got out. Of course, we were told the prosecutor could always appeal, but the lawyers would try. Meanwhile, Daniel took French lessons. If you learned French, your sentence would be reduced by a few months.

Miriam and Daniel saw miracles daily. All prisoners received one baguette (a crusty loaf of bread) daily, which was kosher. His first Friday in prison, Daniel was depressed at not having what he needed to bring in Shabbos and say a proper Kiddush. Friday morning, when handed his daily loaf of bread, he mused that if only he had another loaf he would have the two loaves he needed for Shabbos.

Almost immediately, the guard reappeared. "Hey," he said to Daniel, "I have an extra loaf. Do you want it?"

Later that week, while cleaning his cell, Daniel noticed a full can of Coke lying at the bottom of his window ledge. It had probably fallen from someone's outside "fridge." (Prisoners kept food cold by hanging it in a bag outside their windows.) He tried to reach it through his tiny window opening, but gave up after a while and went back to saying his morning prayers. When he was done, he turned around to find the can waiting for him at the top of his window.

Letters were Daniel's lifeline. He saved every one he received and reread them constantly. One day Daniel's roommate lost it. In his own loneliness, lacking contact with the outside world, he attacked Daniel and threw Daniel's portfolio of letters out the window.

Though Daniel only restrained him, the incident was seen by the guards as a fight. Fighting meant immediate solitary confinement for them both. And so Daniel spent Simchas Torah stripped and isolated in a small cell. His depression worsened at the thought of his lost letters.

Meanwhile, unbeknown to Daniel, an Arab prisoner Daniel had befriended saw the letters flying all over the yard. He picked them up, even going into restricted areas to do so, and returned them all, every one, to Daniel. Daniel felt that the reason for the Arab's kindness was because a while before he had noticed Daniel using computerized address labels. We had sent these to him. The man had asked Daniel if he could get him some — prisoners hated writing their back address with the many numbers (cell number, prisoner number, address number) over and over. At Daniel's request, we had sent some labels to this Arab. Perhaps it was our act of kindness that motivated this prisoner to save Daniel's letters. If so, it had certainly been worth the effort.

The prison warden questioned Daniel about the fight. He asked why Daniel was so scratched up and bruised and his roommate was not. Daniel explained that all he wanted to do was protect himself, and so all he did was restrain his roommate, not hurt him. The attack had been an act of temporary insanity, not personal aggression. Why should he hurt the guy?

The warden confessed that restraining someone half your size who attacks you instead of severely beating him was not a common situation in prison. He said he would be sure to tell the judge about it, as it might help.

And there were so many more miracles.

Miriam and Daniel prayed for food, and it somehow came. A shofar miraculously showed up in the music room where the Jewish prisoners were allowed to pray on Rosh HaShanah. My daughter had said to me, "I don't know why G-d wanted us to go through this, to be in here. But He is holding our hands all the time."

16
Dear Daddy

Hi Daddy,

I just came back to my room from seeing Mom, so she'll send you my love, but then I thought that I'll write to you.

My day here is pretty routine. We are woken up at 7:00 by the surveillantes, nurse-like guards, have breakfast, and empty our garbage cans into a larger bin. Breakfast is a three-packet thing with milk powder, coffee, and sugar, and here in the nursery we're also given a dairy product like yogurt or fromage frais (some sour cream/yogurt type of thing). The fromage frais has a hechsher on it. On Monday, Wednesday, and Friday we have showers. Then we're free till 9:00 to clean our rooms, make beds, eat, etc. I daven.

At 9:00 we can go out to the courtyard if we want for two hours. I usually am only up to Shema in shacharis so I stay to finish davening. Then at about 11:30 or 12:00 lunch comes. They give an appetizer, main dish, and dessert. Also here in the nursery we get a liter of milk or two yogurts or some type of dairy supplement. The appetizer or dessert is often

58

a fruit, so I can eat it. But the main meal comes in a metal TV dinner tray and is SO treif. It's often meat and milk in one meal! No pork, though, since there is a large Muslim population here.

There is a canteen where you can buy food and supplies, so I bought dishes and cutlery and food. I bought a stove. I should receive it on Friday. I'll be able to cook rice, couscous, eggs, etc. on it.

The rabbi has brought me food twice. Meals in tin cans and cheeses and nosh and matzah. Both times it was a nes from Hashem. The first time I had not yet been able to buy any food and was getting very concerned about the baby because it needs lots of nourishment and I wasn't eating as much as I should've been. Suddenly the rabbi brings lots of cheeses and meats and drinks so I was, thank G-d, set until I received my canteen products. Then last week I was supposed to get my kosher foods on Tuesday, but they didn't show up. On Wednesday I was low on food, and I asked Hashem to help me. Within the hour I received a box with matzah, meals, candy, and cheese from the rabbi. Again I was saved!

On Friday morning I was upset that I wouldn't have anything special for Shabbos, and I told Hashem that I would appreciate my kosher canteen. Well, it came that day as well. So, thank G-d, the baby and I are being fed by hand from Hashem. The rabbi also brought me sefarim which I finished on Shabbos, and a calendar. He has really been great. He also went through the canteen with me to show me what is kosher.

There is also a nun here who has been a big help (and an inspiration) for me. Not only has she provided me with paper, pens, stamps, a dictionary, and a sweatshirt, and will also give me a textbook to learn French, but she has also been a source of good spirit. She's optimistic and kind and caring. She visits me often, sometimes just to say hello. I think we inspire each other to continue our belief in the good.

After lunch we are given another opportunity to go outside, this time in the main courtyard. It's much noisier there, but I go sometimes and take a book or my Tehillim, just to get out of my room and outside. That's from 2:00–4:00. You can go in at 3:00 and usually I do. I come in and say minchah, then nap till supper at 5:30 to 6:00.

Then I make my supper — sandwiches with tuna or sardines or avocado or sometimes one of the meals from the rabbi. The canteen sells these meals as well. Then I finish my Tehillim for the day and daven minchah if I didn't already. I often sing to the baby. Songs like "Ani Ma'amin," "Ana BeKoach," "Mizmor LeDavid," all good songs with wonderful meanings. I clean my room from supper, prepare for bed, do some laundry...

This is when time moves VERY slowly. You can't daven at night till after 9:30, and since I have no watch yet (we're working on it) I wait till it's dark, then daven maariv, count sefirah, say Shema, and go shluffy. In between I write letters.

Oops, they just called me to go speak with the psychologist. She's from the hospital where, if I'm here, I'll have the baby. She came once before. She's nice and speaks a bit of English.

Well, that was fun! She's a nice lady. She'll come again. She wants to have a group with all the pregnant ladies to talk to each other.

I hope the rabbi comes today. They didn't allow Mom to give me your Tanach. Oh, your Zaidy's name was Menachem? Bubby Rochel's father? The one you learned with? I want to check on all our names in the family (for baby names), boys and girls. If you could, let me know some of our family's names and who they were and what was special about them. A big job, I know.

Did you finish that textbook for your course? I hope you're sleeping better. I know it's hard because there are so many unanswered questions. But rely on Hashem. Say your prayers and do your best to "serve G-d in joy!" Just like we accept His judgments when they're good (in our eyes), so too we should accept the ones that appear bad in our eyes with the same faith in Hashem that He is GOOD!

The nursery is more like a hospital than a prison. It's very nice. Our courtyard has beautiful roses and some other flowers. You see and hear little children playing. They stay here until they're eighteen months old, then go to family.

Well, in a week Mom will be leaving France and be back home and soon after that we'll hear from the judge!! We'll know where we stand in this. Well, at least we are safe, physically and emotionally and spiritually. So that should be a comfort to you. We are healthy and growing in ruchniyus. We've matured from this, are less naive and more responsible. So there's lots of good from this already. My husband is even being mekarev his roommate!

Well, that's about all. Oh, I wear my own clothes, even my sheitel! At night I wear my snood and tuck away the sheitel till the morning. Only one person asked what it was. I explained that it's a hat! Also I just made a leichter for Shabbos, so I'm lighting oil neiros now. I feed my leftover bread to the birds who visit my window. They're very appreciative.

I have the pictures you sent hanging in my room and it's very nice to look around and see family and friends. Mom did laundry for me. I should be getting that back today with the pictures from the special album you made. So I'll have even more family and friends to look at. I also have some of your letters hanging. The one with the babies all over it and the one with your picture. You look very nice! I also have a picture of you and Mom from your wedding. You both look good there, too.

Well, I'll mail this tonight so you should get it when Mom returns! I think France is in its own time warp. Everything is in slow motion. I'll write another snail mail letter soon.

Lots and lots of hugs and kisses and love,
From your baby and her baby

17
The Rabbi, the Nun — an Incredible Duo

T he "stove" Miriam ordered turned out to be a device similar to the heating trays caterers use. Meanwhile Daniel learned to make his own "prison stove." It consisted of three soda cans holding up a can of sardines with the oil from the sardines in it. "Light it," he told me with the pride of someone who just mastered a new skill, "and you can warm stuff and just about have enough time to cook pasta." He wrote my daughter the instructions so that she should make one, too, and use it until her "stove" came.

Meanwhile, she was working on what to name her baby. It was easier to think of names than the horror of having a baby in prison.

The rabbi and the nun were incredible people, an incredible duo. Through them I had been able to see my daughter on Fridays in place of the Saturday appointment, and I even had a visit once on a Thursday when Shavuos was on Friday. I had been in France three weeks. I had seen my daughter six times. Without those two angels it would have been much, much less.

The nun was from Ireland, and she spoke fluent English and French with the heaviest Irish accent I had ever heard. The rabbi, who visited the prison weekly, spoke no English, and I needed to communicate through his daughter. His whole family was warm and helpful and always available to us.

The nun lived on the prison grounds and, with a few other fellow clergy, serviced the prison. It was her life's work. She was warm and kind and had a wonderful sense of humor. I will always remember the day we met her. She had arranged our first non–visiting day visit. She looked out for my son and me and helped us as we spoke no French. The guards, for the most part, chose to speak no English.

We were carrying my daughter's clean laundry. (If laundry was not taken by visitors, the prisoners had to do it by hand. If they had money they could buy soap and a wooden dryer, making it a bit easier.) We got off the bus after our usual endless ride on two trains and a bus and started walking to the women's prison.

Suddenly it started to rain, a real downpour. I put the clean laundry package I carried over my head as a makeshift umbrella. "Please, G-d," I said, "could we have five more minutes without rain just to get there dry?"

Miraculously the rain instantly stopped.

A fellow passenger who had exited the bus with us overheard my plea. Perhaps thinking himself funny, he looked at me, smiled, then looked up at the heavens and said, "Thanks, Mother Nature."

Instantly the heavens opened again, and though he quickly apologized, the damage was done, and the downpour continued.

We approached the prison and saw a nun in full habit wearing a bright yellow rain slicker. "'Ello," she said with a wonderful warm smile, outstretched hand, and heavy Irish accent that would put a smile on anyone's face. I thanked her for all the things she had done and for helping my daughter keep her spirits up. I especially thanked her for helping arrange these non–visiting day visits. She sloughed it off.

"T'was nothing," she said. "Glad to help you and Mike" (as she called my daughter). "But you must remember I can't help you with the Sabbath or Holy Day visits without it coming from the rabbi first. It looks a little odd to my superiors, you see," and she laughed, "if it starts with me, you see, instead of the rabbi." And she laughed that contagious twinkle of a laugh once again. "Have a nice visit. I'll see you when you're done."

She took us through the same place we had gone for each visit, but it was so much easier now. We just followed her, as she spoke us through in her French that sounded more like Irish. No clanging locked doors or keys jingling.

It had been arranged that we meet my daughter in the lawyer's room instead of the usual visiting room. It had a wooden table and real chairs. It was more informal and you could smoke here (which pleased my son). But the best was that no guards were constantly passing by, jingling their keys and clicking the locks. What a welcome change! Amazing, how small niceties become wonderful happenings.

She helped us, this nun, in so many ways. She was always there for "Mike," visiting her daily, getting her a maternity outfit until the package I sent arrived, and so much more. She always respected my daughter as a practicing Jewess and never crossed boundaries.

After our visit, which "somehow" had miraculously been about ninety minutes instead of an hour, we saw the sister again. We were still soaked from the rain. She took us into a visiting room in the "community" where the Christian clergy lived. She made us some hot tea and invited us to wait there anytime we came. The weather was often cold or raining. We could just let ourselves in, she said, and feel free to use the washroom. "It's clean, you see, and I've seen the visitors' washroom in the prison, you see. No need to wait outside in the cold. These visits are hard enough on people."

She took Miriam's watch from me. It miraculously appeared in my daughter's cell the next day. Over tea she told us the funniest story. It seemed that a cell phone had been ringing late at night in the women's prison. As no phones were allowed, the entire prison had been searched, but the phone was not found. The next night the phone was heard again, and another fruitless search of the prisoners and their cells ensued. It seems, the nun told us, that one of the prisoners had recorded the sound of a phone ringing on her tape recorder and was tormenting the guards into thinking someone had a phone and was getting calls in the middle of the night.

When the sister found out how we had come, she told us of a direct bus. It went straight from the center of town to the prison and would save us over two hours of traveling time — not to mention the comfort it would give us, with its padded reclining seats. She took out her schedule and discovered one was leaving in five minutes. What a sight we were, a woman, a young man, and a nun in a yellow raincoat running through the rain to catch the bus. All the while, the sister waved her hands and yelled at the bus to wait for us in her Irish French.

She gave me her phone number when I was leaving France and told me to call her as often as I liked and she'd give me a report on "Mike." She'd be sure to see her every day if she could. "Lovely girl," she said. "We all know she doesn't belong here. The warden knows it, too, and we're all a bit protective of her, you see."

I wanted to make a donation to her order to express my thanks. She refused. "Give it to the rabbi," she said, "so it will help him to continue to do what he can for the people here too."

Months later I received a call from the sister. "No, no, nothing's wrong, you see, Mike's doing fine. I just called to let you know I'm going on a bit of a holiday for three weeks, and I was worried that if you should call and not get me, no one would be able to tell you in English what's up, you see. I don't want you to worry."

Two minutes later the phone rang again. "Foolish me," she said, "I forgot to give you a message from your daughter. She sends her love. She and the baby to be are feeling fine, don't you worry. I'll speak to you when I return. Here are the dates. I promise I'll see Mike as soon as I return. I have the keys, you see."

When I offered to reimburse her for the calls, she told me not to worry, saying it was a gift from the prison. It was just that the prison didn't know it. This nun had quite the habit.

The rabbi, who visited the prison approximately once a week, came with kosher food, treats, books, smiles, and good cheer. He would fax us a note from Miriam immediately after his visit so that we could hear news of her the same day. How we treasured those faxes!

I found out later that initially, Miriam went out only in the morning to the nursery promenade in the smaller courtyard that was only for pregnant prisoners and prisoners with young children. She had been afraid to go out in the afternoon into the regular yard. She was fearful of taking someone's spot or antagonizing fellow inmates. Because of her refusal to go out in the afternoon, a social worker was sent to check her for depression. She insisted Miriam go outside for fresh air in the afternoon and get out of her hot, humid cell or take antidepressants.

Not wanting to inflict medication on her baby, Miriam finally ventured out. She found the inmates of the larger prison not frightening, but friendly and helpful, as they had been in the nursery.

She often chatted with the English-speaking girls, from Canada, the United States, Israel, and England. They helped each other, shared their sadness and frustration over the "French system" and their anger at being there. She, too, was now part of a community, a community of prisoners.

Until last month, we had never even given people in these circumstances a single thought. And, until last month, we never thought we would ever have anything to do with prisons and inmates.

18
I'm Doing Fine

Thursday
(Flowers for the Holidays)

Dear Daddy,

This morning it has been very rainy. Kinda not-good-mood weather. But your letters, as usual, cheered me up. Your graphics and corny jokes just bring that big smile right back to my face.

Well, I've been reading in pregnancy books that all my "symptoms" are normal. Baruch Hashem, I was lucky and had almost no morning sickness. But I do have some headaches, gas, heartburn, etc., and lots of joy thinking about the baby and even more when I see the pictures of the family and I think about sharing this bundle of joy with everyone. I'm in my fifteenth week — my fourth month. I'll let you know the moment I feel it move. I haven't yet.

I'm looking forward to seeing Mom and Josh today. It always is helpful. Monday, though, will be our last visit before Mom goes home. But soon, in a week or two, we should hear from the lawyer with what the judge says!! Maybe the baby's first movements will be felt at home! Let's ask G-d for the best.

Daniel met another Jew in prison. He used to be frum, but since he's been in prison (forty-month sentence! Ouch!) he lost his faith. So Daniel's warming him up. We may find my husband's calling yet!! He can join our chaplain in the chaplain business!

I received cards and letters from many friends and one from Mrs. Goldberg (the mother of our "friend" who asked us to take the suitcase). She is very heartbroken. I also received mail from Daniel's rosh yeshivah and his wife. It was a short note saying they sent me a new release by Rabbi Krohn — but I guess the prison guy wanted to read it first, so he's keeping it. I'll ask about it soon.

Please, let people know how helpful it is to get mail and give them Daniel's address as well. I'm going to ask Mom about writing to Bubby. If she thinks it's okay, I'll send her a letter right away. I'm not sure of her zip code. I'll ask Mom to get it for Monday if she can.

As Mom and Josh probably told you, France is not wheelchair friendly. Stairs everywhere! So I pray I'll come to you (soon). Please let me know how Uncle Sol is doing. Also please keep me updated on my kallah teacher. She's expecting and her nephew is the sick two-year-old I asked you to say Tehillim for. Please let me know how he is.

I'll finish this letter after I see Mom and company. Love ya lots. Keep those smiles coming!!

Hi Pops! — aka Grandpops!

Well, I'm back from my visit with Mom and Josh. It was great. I'm always cheery after a visit. I sent love with them and wishes for a good yom tov. They told me about the idea to keep our apartment. I'd rather our rent money go to our large outstanding bill. That would be much better. I don't plan on being in that apartment again. I'm planning to discuss it all with Daniel when I write him tomorrow.

Our friends can do all our packing for us within a few days. They do not need any supervision as was suggested. I trust them more than anyone else. They are welcome to help pack up. I don't know all their phone numbers, but I'm enclosing the ones I do know and they can give you the others' numbers. If you speak with our friends, they'll arrange it. So that's a start at least.

If my friend Batya wants to do the kitchen, that's great. I'm sure she'll be meticulous with packing the dishes carefully. Please ask my friend Sheila to take my kesubah. It's in the top left drawer of our dresser in the bedroom. This is most important! I trust her with it. Okay?

That's all the business stuff. I need to write to Daniel to okay it all with him. That apartment is nothing but a drain on our (and the families') very limited resources. We do not and will not need it. We should clear out and not pay one more penny of rent. The money, any money, should pay our bills and the expenses of this mess. Okay?

I just wrote to Daniel. Josh is going to see him tomorrow and so I'll have an idea of what he thinks. Otherwise I'll have to wait till the end of next week when a letter comes.

Well, I didn't daven minchah yet, so I'm gonna do that now and say some Tehillim. Oh, if you speak to the Goldbergs, please tell them that neither of us is angry at them. Daniel wrote to them early on and he was very scared and angry, especially for my sake and the baby. We don't blame them for any of this. They should try to get their son to help us in any way he can.

Mom tells me that maybe he'll sign saying we didn't know the package had drugs. I don't know if it will help, but he must do whatever he can to help us. It's in his hands, not his parents. I have no negative feelings towards them. I understand their position is very hard. Please tell them we still love them and hope to share many more simchahs with them. I'm short on stamps this week, but as soon as I can, I will write to them.

Thanks, Daddy-o. I've given you a few jobs. Okay, mail time!

Love ya lots,
Your daughter

19
Waiting Game

I had come to France armed with books about pregnancy and was glad to see the information Miriam read was helping to keep her calm and positive. Though the care in the prison was adequate, the doctor rarely spoke to her, and it seemed useless to ask questions. Miriam would plead for a copy of the sonogram to send to Daniel, who would then send it to us. We'd copy it, enlarge it, and send it and the original back to them in prison. There it was hung on my daughter's wall with the other family photos.

The "*parloir*," or "powwows" as my children called them, did not always go smoothly.

On one visit to my son-in-law, we were locked in the visiting room as usual. All the prisoners arrived, but not Daniel. We waited and knocked on the door, but got no response. With every waiting moment, our fear that something had happened to him intensified.

Finally he arrived fifteen minutes late. They had neglected to tell him he had visitors. He had started his morning prayers when they came to get him and could not stop until he was finished. And we were sitting in our cubicle waiting, not knowing what had happened.

Worse still, we had lost fifteen precious minutes of our thirty-minute time slot.

We have no control over the actions of our adult children. We are not responsible for what they do, yet are often assigned blame. I was amazed at my daughter's ability to separate her feelings of hurt and betrayal toward their "friend," who used them to transport his drugs, from her feelings toward his family. His parents had no idea what he had done or of his involvement in the drug ring. Daniel and Miriam had been so close to them all. His siblings were like their own siblings and his parents, their second set of parents, whom they loved dearly. They had practically lived in their house. I was amazed that Miriam could continue to love his parents and siblings while feeling intense anger towards him.

His parents called us often. The pain they felt over what their son had done was palpable, and they repeatedly begged our forgiveness. They were trying to get him to sign an affidavit that stated Miriam and Daniel had no idea that drugs were in the suitcase. Fearing his own arrest, he refused. Instead he ran off to Israel and made himself difficult to find. How hard they tried to find him, how hard they worked towards getting this affidavit I'll never know. How hard would I try, in their place, if it meant a jail term for him in exchange for possible freedom for Daniel and Miriam?

We were shocked when the lawyers told us not to have any further contact with this family, as it could harm our case and endanger our children. I'd never before had any experience with a penal system and it never occurred to me then, in my naiveté, what is so obvious to me now — that staying in contact with the family of the perpetrator would make Daniel and Miriam look guilty.

It was very painful for all of us. When his tearful mother called, a few weeks later, I told her we had to stop all contact with her family. She reluctantly accepted our decision, but the pain in her voice reflected my own sorrow. The harm was done. The pieces would never be put together again.

We waited to hear from the judge. Her assessment of the case was crucial, pivotal. She held Miriam and Daniel's future in her hands: release or trial, guilt or naiveté. We all kept hoping to hear her decision any day.

The anticipation stretched on and on, into days and weeks. We waited. Maybe this month...maybe today...maybe tomorrow...maybe...

20
Risks and Reality

Miriam had prepared a tiny piece of paper with phone numbers for me. Phone numbers she wouldn't remember by heart, of friends to call to help clear out her apartment. She had hidden the paper in her waistband. Nothing was allowed to be passed to a visitor or received from one. Prisoners were summarily searched after each visit, but usually just patted down before. The option was there for heavier searches before visitations at the discretion of the guards.

She had passed me slips of paper once before, slipping them into my clothing while we hugged. I had begged her not to do it, fearing the consequences, but to Miriam, it seemed like a high school prank. Something to get away with when all else was restricted.

That day, before our visit, they found the paper. She was allowed my visit. She chose not to tell me about the incident. I was to discover later that she was visited by a guard with a translator shortly after the visit. She was informed that visits from then on would take place in a room with a glass divider and a telephone for communication. No hugs or kisses or touching would be possible. Further, the judge who was reviewing her file and whose responsibility it was to review the case would be informed of her flagrant disregard for prison rules. Through tears and pleas, she somehow got the guard to relent and give her another opportunity to prove herself.

She thought later it might have been her wall covered with family photos that the guard kept looking at that may have softened his resolve. Maybe it was the picture of her and her dad in his wheelchair that the translator asked about. Or maybe it was plain luck. Or maybe it was Divine intervention. Either way, the judge would not be informed this time. Visitations would continue as they had, for now.

At that point, my daughter began to grow in years, by minutes. This was not a high school prank. This was prison. There were real consequences that could change your life, could threaten your future as soon as tomorrow.

Hi.

Well, a man just came to ask me about my note that I had written and tried to take in to my visit with Mom, so I wouldn't forget what to tell her during our visit. He was very understanding. I explained the note to him and he said that I can't write down stuff and take notes to visits and this is my last warning. After this, it goes to the judge and powwows are through a window. He asked why my dad wasn't here, so I told him and showed him a picture and he understood. He was very kind and said this was my first and last warning. Thank G-d. I'll never do that again.

Love ya! ♡
Your daughter

21
Our Unrealistic Timeframe

Monday

Hi Daddy,

I just got back from my last visit with my precious family and tomorrow they'll be on their way home. Please wish our friends the Burtons mazal tov on the bar mitzvah and on their son's engagement. I guess you'll get this when Mom comes back. Well, it's one month and a day from your anniversary (34 years?)! Maybe we'll have a great surprise for your anniversary and we'll make a big party! Oh, I hope so! I sent hugs and kisses with Mom, but with G-d's help, I'll give them to you personally.

It's gonna to be a slow few weeks till we hear from the lawyer. I guess we just gotta wait some more till we find out where we stand.

Okay, I just had a little cry. I miss you guys a lot. Well, now I feel better. It was easier not to miss you when I knew I would see Mom or Josh, but now the reality hits again. Poor Mommy has to go home without her baby. I'm sure that it's breaking her heart all over again.

75

This is tough for us all on different levels.

Try to be a bit strong for Mom and for yourself, too. We'll come through this stronger people, Pops! But only if we do our best! So trust in G-d and we'll be fine. Hashem takes care of us. He's already holding our hands, and soon He'll lead us out of here. Soon! But we've got to be strong while we wait. Like the postcard you sent me said. Believe in yourself, believe in the strength you have deep inside, believe in tomorrow and what it will bring… You, too, and grow with the flow. I like that, Dad, it's good.

Anyway, I'm pooped from today. We got up at 7:00 for our showers and I need a nap or I won't make it till dark to daven. I wrote to my friend Sheila. I forgot to ask her to take my kesubah to her house. Mom is going to ask her to organize a pack-up for our apartment. Our friends are certainly there for us. Unfortunately, it's necessary. There are so many loose ends of our life that need to be dealt with.

Please send my love to all of our friends. I hope you had or (if this miraculously gets to you before) have a great time at the bar mitzvah. Please send the Burtons our love too. Oh, tell your friend, Rosie, that I'm due the first two weeks of November. Maybe the Burtons can try to make the wedding before that, if possible, so I can attend.

Well, that's it for today. I love you guys lots and I miss you almost as much. Please G-d, we'll be together soon. At home or in Israel with Mashiach.

Love you,
Your daughter and the little neshamaleh

This letter arrived on two different colored bits of paper remnants, with the unused part torn off and saved for the next letter. I could only assume the canteen had not arrived, and she was afraid that she would run out of paper.

I was glad the supportive cards and notes we had collected to send them were helping. We tried to be upbeat and positive in our letters, talking of concerns and troubles only when unavoidable, or when we needed the children's input.

I was beginning to realize just how unrealistic our time line had been. But my daughter still clung to the belief that her baby would not be born in prison and she might even attend an upcoming friend's wedding after the birth of her baby.

22
Going Home without My Daughter

Dear Dad,
 Saw Miriam today. She sends her love and says she will continue to write as often as possible. Hope all is well there. By the time you get this, we will probably be home and you can see all of our pictures, not just this lousy postcard.
                                                                Love ya lots,
                                                                Your son, Josh

We had been in France for a month. We were going home without my daughter and son-in-law.

During my last visit with my daughter I had an overwhelming desire to reach across the table that separated us and take her with me, take her home. I was leaving my twenty-one-year-old pregnant daughter in a prison in France for who knows how long. I was beyond pain. I was numb. This whole thing was still unreal.

We had traveled so far and spent so many hours traveling from one prison to the other, meeting with lawyers and employees of the embassy and doing everything we could to get this nightmare to end. For the last month, that had been the shape or our lives. Exhaustion mingled with depression as I willed one foot in front of the other.

We traveled to the airport. I was scheduled to meet my husband at the Minneapolis airport. From there my son would fly home and return to his job and his routine as best he could. I was to travel to Illinois where my closest friend of thirty years was having a bar mitzvah for one son and an engagement party for another.

Was I crazy? Did I want to do this? Could I do this? These were our dearest friends, who were always there for us, through good times and bad. How could I not show up at their time of joy? What reason could we give if we were absent?

We had told very few people what had happened. We wanted to preserve what privacy we could. How else could our kids eventually resume a normal life? But living a lie, acting as if life was proceeding normally, took an enormous toll on us.

We went to the celebrations. It was the right thing for us to do, after all. It would just test our ability to give and act.

23
Connections Made and Broken

Hi Family!

Today I got the aerograms Mom left for me and the letter and the pictures. Thank you. I have the pictures hanging close to my bed and on my bulletin board with the cards and postcards I've been getting from you guys and my friends. Oh, thanks so much for the vort you sent. It was really nice!

I've gotten letters from so many of my friends. Everyone says how they're all davening for us and they want to help in any way they can. So I've written to them all that we'll need them to pack up our apartment. You'll probably get to them before my letters do.

Well, I managed to cook rice and also an egg (on my "prison stove") without starting a fire. I'll try once again. I've got three more eggs and they're a good source of nutrients, and the rice is good, too, once in a while. I'll leave that till Friday when, I hope, I get my real stove.

We'll hopefully be together soon, perhaps even in a few weeks. As Dad writes to Daniel, "Hashem can save in the blink of an eye." So remember that and don't over strain your eyes by blinking too much!

It's lunchtime now, so I'm going to prepare my lunch and then go play outside. Oh, I got thread and I'm all set with the hair clips! Thank you so much! Oh Dad, you can please send me more divrei Torah. It's great to read them. I also read it to the baby. It's supposed to be able to hear my voice well now. It's learning with its own malach but extra never can hurt. Okay, lunchtime. Love you guys.

Connections. Pictures were her only connections to the outside. Pictures and letters had become her most valued possessions.

Waiting... Waiting for her stove, waiting for her lawyer with news from the judge.

Waiting and trying to be hopeful that this would all end soon. Learning patience through enormous pain.

Hi.

I just had a visit from a lady in the French Jewish community. She's very nice. It was so great to see and speak to a regular frum lady who says "baruch Hashem" and "b'ezras Hashem" and all that. Wow... like recharging my batteries. Well, hopefully these batteries can come out soon! I hope we'll at least know where we stand in a few days. That will at least take the "unknown" part out of this equation. Okay, I'm going to nap now.

I made eggs again and this time it actually worked. My attempt to make a stove like Daniel's last time was a big mess and I was hesitant to do it again, but I have eggs that will go bad if I didn't do something with them. So I tried and this contraption is good. Love you guys lots. Miss you!

Hello there! Well, it's now Sunday morning, 8:15 a.m. I'm eating yogurt, applesauce, and decaf for breakfast. I saw the rabbi on Friday.

The stove I ordered didn't come so I'm gonna try again today. I received confirmation that the mandat cash had cleared so there should be no problems. Who knows, maybe I won't be here Friday to receive it! I hope to hear from the lawyer this week, but I'll try to remain patient. I'll hope for the best while keeping a little "back burner" busy with a picture of the worst.

Well, Thursday and Friday were very hot and sunny days. I could've used some AC. I got a little bit of a tan on my arms and cheeks, but because it's so hot I only stayed out for a short while. Daniel tells me he got a letter from our landlord and others about keeping the apartment. I hear what they're saying. So if we have the opportunity to be home in the next month, it makes sense to keep the apartment. But if not, which is realistic…no one should pay our rent anymore.

Well, my pen died. I'm gonna have to get one from someone. I don't expect this marker to last too long either. Back to important stuff… Why pay rent for two-four-five months when we won't be living there? I hope this gets cleared up soon because each 15th rent is due.

I'm told the landlord won't let anyone but family in to help us move. I'll suggest that we write to our landlord saying who we approve to come in and he can "let" those friends into the apartment to pack for us. This is getting annoying and wasteful already. Of course I would love to go myself, pick out clothes and things, and pack my own stuff and say "bye" to my house, but now I can't do that and I don't think I can do it in June either.

Okay. Enough said, right? I just wish we could speak. It's so annoying to wait eight days till you get a letter, get a mixed message back in between, then respond, etc. I'll send a message with the rabbi, so hopefully by then I'll know what our landlord (actually) said and I'll have answers to all the "problems" of moving out so quickly. Also maybe I'll have heard from the lawyer, but I'm sure he'll keep you up-to-date.

Love,
Miriam and Babes

My daughter and son-in-law asked us to sell their furniture, pack up all their belongings, and give up their apartment. We could not afford the rent on top of the other expenses. They needed a bigger apartment now anyway, with the baby coming. Not knowing how long things would take in France, it seemed the best option. Our hopes of this ending in weeks were ridiculous.

Expenses were adding up. There were disagreements about closing the apartment. Confusion over how to handle the furniture. Questions about who could go in to pack, friends or family. Tension over Miriam and Daniel's plight turned every issue into an argument, with all of us only wanting the nightmare to end. Finally, their belongings were packed and stored, their furniture sold, and the money put away for when they got out of prison, just as they requested. But this happened only after months of delays and disagreements.

Months later, in a bizarre turn of events, we discovered that Miriam's clothing, gathered from her apartment and stored in garbage bags, had all been inadvertently thrown out. Every piece of clothing she owned was gone. Somehow it seemed trivial in light of everything else they had lost. It was only her clothes, after all…just things.

24

All Shades of Blue

Dear Family,

Well, Shabbos was nice — sort of. I was a bit blue at the beginning but finally cheered up. It's sort of pathetic making Shabbos alone and having nothing Shabbosdik. I read a bit of the parashah in the Hebrew/French Chumash, but it's long and I didn't understand it all. It was therefore frustrating rather than uplifting, so I stopped. I had a nice meal. I sang with the baby (no kicking yet). I read. I took a long nap. Then davened minchah, said Pirkei Avos. I have a sefer called Beyond the Letter of the Law which has Pirkei Avos translated and essays which were great to read. Pirkei Avos is easy to translate. It feels good to learn and understand.

Please send more divrei Torah. I share them with the baby and we both enjoy them. I got a letter from the man from CADI saying he hasn't heard any news recently and hopes things are going well and to let him know how I'm doing. On Thursday, when I get more paper, pens, and envelopes, I'll write him a note.

Well, that's about all over here. It's cooler today, baruch Hashem, and Sunday's always a slow day (even slower than usual) because no mail and there are less people around because people leave on the weekend. Not us prisoners! So I'll relax and wait some more. I'm getting a little tired of waiting, but what else can we do? B'ezras Hashem, this will soon be cleared up.

Oh, this lady came back with her newborn. It seems you stay a week in the hospital. Her little girl is so beautiful, with perfect little tiny features. It's so nice to see and gets me more excited (if that's possible)!

The day we were arrested was Daniel's great-grandfather's yahrtzeit. We're contemplating his name as a possibility. I understand he was a great man... Please let me know our family names so I'll make sure we think of them all. I'll send this out at lunch with lots of love!

Hugs and kisses too,
Your (growing up) baby and her (growing) baby!

Not knowing if her canteen would arrive, Miriam had learned to cherish every scrap of paper in order to write letters. The next few envelopes we received contained a variety of large colored confetti, numbered in sequence, each piece having a few sentences written on it. We laid them out in numerical order so that we could read what she had written. At home, these bits of hoarded paper would have been garbage.

We never knew what we could send the prisoners. It was very frustrating, but what made no sense to us often made eminent sense to them. When we were there, we learned that the hard covers of books could be made into knives. The raised letters on book covers could hold drugs. Blue was the color of the guards' uniforms, and so any clothes that were blue were *interdit* for prisoners. Photos could be sent but not given. No magazines or newspapers were allowed, nor were gloves except those that were made of pure wool. Why? We never knew. We'd just line up with everyone else to hand over our items. Some they'd take and some were *"interdit."*

Baby names... She wondered what name to give the baby. In Jewish tradition we name a newborn in honor of a deceased person who exemplifies the strengths of character we desire for our child. She wanted to know everything about every possible choice in order to pick the best match.

On my last visiting day I brought the things she had asked for, a sweatshirt, skirts with elastic waists, and wig clips. I cut the clips out of my wig and put them in an envelope with some bobby pins so the guard would understand that they were hair clips. I was convinced they would be *interdit*, but at least I would try. I would send maternity clothes when I get home, so I could shop more easily and keep the cost down. I threw my French/English dictionary in with everything else, hoping I would never need it again. It had a few phrases written in the front, and I thought it might be of use to Miriam.

To my shock, they accepted it all, and I walked upstairs to the waiting room. Within five minutes, my name was called. The guard motioned that I needed to go back down to the place where I had left all the things for my daughter. *Those clips!*

I was wrong. The dictionary was not allowed because of the phrases I had written in the front! No written messages were allowed. Perhaps they were a secret code.

Miriam sounded so calm in her letter when she wrote about the prisoner's new baby. We were only to learn later what the birthing routine in the prison was, and I wondered how she had managed to sound so composed in her letter.

When a prisoner was in labor, she was taken to the hospital in handcuffs. She remained, guarded of course, in the hospital for five days, and then returned to prison with her baby, if the baby was healthy. The babies stayed with their mothers in prison until eighteen months of age and then had to be given up to a guardian. If a guardian was unavailable or not previously specified, the baby was placed in the hands of social services.

We found out later that inmates often went crazy when their babies were taken from them on the child's eighteenth-month birthday. Once, on just such a day in the yard, one prisoner attacked another, temporarily insane from her hurt and pain. As the prisoners went to break up the fight, my daughter herded the little ones away and tried to calm them. As Miriam's delivery date approached, she would certainly be filled with a mixture of anticipation and dread.

My daughter and son-in-law named me guardian, just in case... None of us ever talked about what it would mean if the guardianship were to be enacted. We just didn't let our thoughts go there. She would give birth in a few months. Eighteen months later, if she was still in prison, I would have to take the baby. I prayed that day would never come.

The day I signed the guardianship papers was the first time I allowed myself to think of the ramifications of what I was doing. It would be best for both mother and child for me to stay in France, so that they could continue to bond. But if I did that, how would I live? Where would I live? Who would care for my handicapped husband? What would happen to my job? It was too much to deal with. I would leave the future where it belonged, in G-d's hands, and I would pray; pray with even more fervor than I had, if that was even possible.

25
Hiding behind Positive Thoughts

Dear Mom, Dad, and Josh:

I ordered a large food supply today. It should arrive a week from today. With G-d's help, I won't be here to get it. Well, the weather finally is beautiful. It rained last night, which cooled it off, but we had three or four days of constant sunshine. It was nice, but hot! So I put a drape up in the window. Sometimes my door is open, which is always better, but it depends on the guard.

One lady's kid was sick and spent a week in the hospital, and she went two times to visit him. He's back now (a four-month-old) and looks great. Another lady had her baby, a beautiful girl. Lots of dark hair, grayish eyes, perfect nose, big full lips. She's a beautiful baby.

Oh, my friend Yael had a baby boy (7.7 lb). I don't know if you remember her, but she's a small, petite girl, so that's a big baby for her. The bris should be this week. I think he was born Wednesday or Thursday night.

My friend Sheila wrote me again. She has my kesubah, so I know where it is and it's safe. I hope those maternity clothes are on their way because I almost can't do up my jean skirt! So I'll be down to one skirt, a dress, and two shirts. I was thinking that if we get out before the summer is over, maybe we'll go camping. I don't know if Daniel has ever camped and it will be fun to show him our campground.

Well, I want to leave some room for tomorrow because I've run out of envelopes. I'll get more on Thursday, but just in case I hear from the lawyer tomorrow, I'll write to you then.

Today was one of the kids' first birthday, so we had a party — cold soda, fruit (which I had), cake, cookies, chips, even gifts. It was nice. Sunday there was a concert — some old dude thinking he was twenty-five (a gift to the world), but it was nice. A bass, violin, keyboard, and a guy with percussion stuff. Sunday is the longest day of the week. No mail, no canteen, just a long day. I have the radio and I found Radio Shalom, and once got Radio J for ten minutes, but I lost the signal.

Okay, it's 5:00 and I must nap for thirty minutes. I'll save the rest for tomorrow and keep you updated.

Love you guys lots.

(The rest of the letter was in dark blue marker.)

Well my pen died but I want to get this out to you today so you'll get it. I know each day without mail is like forever. I got your Mall of America postcard today. Thanks. Thank you for sending the clothes. Perhaps the package will arrive on Friday with the rabbi.

I just came back from the doctor's office. She checked my weight — I've gained 6 kg since arrival. And I heard the heartbeat! It's so cool. A fast whoosh, whoosh like the laundry on high speed. She says everything is fine. Thank G-d.

I don't know when the next echograph will be, but she gave me one of the old ones from May 4, so I'm sending it to Daniel and he'll send you the one he has, which is the same time just a different pose.

Well, that's all for today. I'm gonna rest/nap now (it's 4:20) till supper comes.

Lots of love,
Your daughter and her baby

Descriptions of beautiful babies and the miracle of birth. She was hiding in positive thoughts, blanking out the rest, just as an overweight person only sees his face in a full-length mirror.

Camping. We had always gone camping in the summer. Memories of happier, freer times.

Clothes. I had sent her a huge package of maternity clothes, everything from nightgowns to shirts and tops and jackets. I was told it would arrive in a week. She needed the clothes badly. Where, how would she get clothes in prison in the meantime?

As it turned out, my parcel did not arrive. A baby does not stop growing while the post office searches for a missing package. I shopped again and sent another box of clothes, which eventually did arrive. The first package made its way to France several months later. Miriam was in her eighth month when it finally turned up.

26
Megavitamins for the Heart

Dear Mama and Papa:

No news from the lawyers yet. We're still anxiously waiting. I got new paper, pens, and envelopes, so my letters will be coming more often, one a day, like a vitamin.

Today (and yesterday) is cool, which is nice, because most of my clothes are suited to this weather! Today I'm wearing the sweatshirt you got me when you were here. Thanks again.

Well, it seems like this apartment thing is getting confusing. The arguments to keep it are mostly for ease of coming "home" and also sentimental ones. Of course I would love nothing more than to leave France (ASAP) and go to my own home with welcoming friends, but if that isn't a possibility for more than past August, then I don't think it should be continued. Once we hear from the lawyer, we'll know better where we stand and when we'll be leaving France. Please explain this to everyone who insists we keep our apartment. I'd like to spend some time in your home when this is done, even have the baby there if possible.

I finally got my "stove" today and two pots, a bowl, and the fuel for the stove. It's like a heating thing used for parties, but it's just in time, because I have rice, pasta, couscous, veggies, eggs, and falafel waiting, and my kosher canteen was rejected. I'm going to ask the rabbi to bring me some food for the next two weeks till I can order again. Plus I'm going to ask the lawyer to put more money in my account. The stove was a big but necessary expense, almost 200 francs! But from now till I leave (soon, with G-d's help), I'll only need money for food.

Well, I'm at the end of the page. I hope you're getting my letters. Have a great Shabbos, and with G-d's help, we'll be together for the next one! Send Josh my love and hugs and kisses for all of you.

Love,
Your daughter and baby

P.S. I heard the baby's heart beating yesterday! It's so fast!

This letter came on normal writing paper. I knew she had gotten her canteen and at least had some food in her cupboard along with the pens and paper.

My heart sank when she had previously mentioned that she would write once a week to save on the cost of stamps and paper. She was always conscious of what this was costing us. How could she know how I waited for the mailman every day? How precious a letter from her was. I would take it out of the mailbox and just hold it. I absorbed it, kissed it, read it, and reread it. Just seeing the envelope in my mailbox worked as a tranquilizer, calming me, telling me she was still okay, alive, and able to write. Irrational fears flourish in irrational situations.

I immediately wrote and begged for daily mail, even two words. Her response was daily mail, volumes of it. I loved it. Megavitamins for the heart.

We were trying to follow their wishes and instructions about their apartment, furniture, and belongings. We understood being imprisoned meant having all your independence stolen and not being allowed to make a decision. I was concerned that this psychological imprisonment could impair their ability to lead a normal life later on, so my husband and I followed their instructions and wishes fully and involved them in every decision we could.

With snail mail our only communication, it was tedious and drawn out, but it was the only way we could give them some freedom when they had none. Unfortunately, living far away from their home made us dependent on others. It hurt me so when people overrode their wishes and instructions. All I could think of was how further imprisoned it would make them feel.

My son had taught me to do a "*mandat cash*" when we were in France. It is a French money order and the only way of getting money to prisoners. The lawyer sent the money once we left France and was reimbursed. I was worried that Miriam might be reluctant to ask for money when she needed it. I tried to encourage her not to go without, but she knew we had been to France, rented a room, traveled to see her, bought her maternity clothes and books. She knew the money had to come from somewhere. She knew it was money we didn't have, and so she was careful, perhaps too careful, spending it.

When each letter arrived, I'd call my son at work and my husband in his office to share it. We all hung on to Miriam's every word. It didn't matter how many times she repeated the weather report, her menu, and her routine. It was all we had to hold on to. To us it was precious.

27
Fear and Frustration

Dear Mom and Dad,

Well, Shabbos was pretty nice. My davening was, thank G-d, great. I davened Friday night to the tunes we do at home. I got my "stove" Friday, so I cooked all day. I made rice with fried veggies, falafel patties instead of balls, eggs, couscous, and pasta. My meals this Shabbos were very nice.

No kicks from your grandkid yet, although I may just not be noticing them. The books say in first pregnancies the woman often doesn't notice the slight movements because we don't know what it feels like. Well, by next Shabbos I should have definite baby movements because the kid is strong enough to move and kick hard enough that I'll have no question that it's the baby. Maybe by then we'll be home!

Well, we're still waiting even more anxiously to hear from the lawyer. Oh, I still didn't write to Bubby. I figured I'd wait, but it seems like I'm still waiting, so could you send me her zip code. Please assure her I'm doing well (with G-d's help). Okay? We'll hear from the lawyer within this week and I'll write to her. She'll get my letter eventually.

Well, with your trip to the bar mitzvah, the daily letters certainly were missed. But I got your postcards. The second one arrived on Shabbos. I made French toast today for lunch but without an egg because my last egg had two blood spots.[2] It was strange, but tasted good. I wrote to the lawyer on Friday.

When the rabbi comes I hope I'll get the clothes that were sent. They should've arrived in France last week, but the rabbi didn't come this past week. I hope everything is all right with him and his family. The weather is still cool, so I'm well clothed for now. I guess spring is not the best time to visit France; the weather is so varied from minute to minute.

So Mom, did you take photos of France to show Dad? When I get home, I'll develop mine and we'll compare. Well, it's 4:00 now. My naptime. I try very hard to nap until 5:30, because otherwise I don't make it to 11:00 to daven — and we thought sunset at home was late! Wow, how I'd love to be home.

Oh, I'm not sure if I told you, but Daniel and I decided to use only chalav Yisrael milk and eat pas Yisrael. Obviously we're not able to do that in prison, but, as soon as we're able, we'd like to do this.

Do you feel there is any danger in us going back to our home? I've been trying to think about it, but I'll trust Josh's and Aaron's opinion. So ask Josh what he thinks and when he feels it would be safe for us to go back. More than ever, our old neighborhood is our home, and, G-d willing, we'd like to return there as soon as we can.

After we get released from prison I'd like to come to you to see you guys and lay low and recuperate from our "vacation." Once we know when we'll be out of here, we'll need to set up a job for Daniel. That's something very important. Until then, do you have any ideas of what he

---

2. A blood spot in an egg makes that egg not kosher.

could do? I think I'll be able to style wigs. It's not going to bring in much money. I can't charge big city prices, but at least it's something.

Well, this is all hypothetical, because we may be in France for the next few months (G-d forbid). So we'll just have to wait to hear from the lawyer. Until then, these are all just ideas that I've been having. Let me know what you think, okay? I really better nap now.

So… See ya soon, my wonderful family (with G-d's help).

Love,

Your kid and the grandkid-to-be

P.S. Mom, when is your eye surgery? Is it this week? You're in my prayers every day!

Send love to Aunt Martha/Izzie, Meshulem, etc.

Maybe this will help pass the time.

And she enclosed a picture of an hourglass.

My mother was eighty-eight. She and my daughter had a special relationship. They lived in the same city. I lived far, far away and Miriam had taken on my role as caregiver, calling my mom often, visiting and having her over whenever she would come. My mom was very worried about them.

Still, her reaction to what happened surprised me. She was more angry than depressed. She couldn't understand how someone who was supposedly religious could do such a thing. She was going to go find their "friend," the one who had set them up, and cut off his tzitzis. She couldn't understand why the police didn't believe her grandchildren and didn't just go out and arrest the other guy. She knew her grandchildren would never deal in drugs. Didn't the police understand this?!

I tried to explain. Miriam and Daniel had told the police all they knew. Arrests had been made. Each arrest had led to another. She asked me if they would be in danger if they returned to their home. I was definitely out of my realm of experience or expertise, but I counseled caution. First things first, though. They needed to be free.

As I read Miriam's letter, I could feel her fear and frustration over having no one with whom to discuss her pregnancy. Was what she was feeling and not feeling normal or cause for concern? There is so much first-time mothers learn just from talking with their friends or calling their moms and sharing experiences. This had been stolen from her.

Unknowns are the worst forms of fears.

I could identify with her constant desire for news about her case in the slow-moving legal system. I could identify with her constant desire for information, her pain in not knowing what her situation was. We could only communicate through letter, and by the time she'd receive ours, or Josh's, or the lawyer's, the news was stale.

28
The Routine Continues

Dear Mom, Dad, and Josh:

Hi there, family. Well, I'm still here! The rabbi came today. He says he'll fax you tonight and tell you how I'm doing. I sent my love with him. The lawyer sent a note that says he'll come this week and he put money in my account. Well, hopefully I'll see him and his partner tomorrow 'cuz I'm going nuts waiting for news. Once he tells us what the judge says, then we'll know where we stand. Even if we have to stay in prison for a little, at least we'll know when this ends.

I have a tiny voice in my head saying that the judge did something to push off giving any real answer and we're in the same boat with a bunch of unanswered questions. But I'm hopeful and I trust that G-d is taking care of us. This has an end. We just can't see it. With G-d's help, we'll see the end soon.

My friends continue to send cards and letters and pictures and encouragement and love, and it's so nice to know that Daniel and I have wonderful friends waiting for us. They all say the same thing. They're davening for our speedy return. Our old neighborhood isn't the same without us, and everyone misses us. Well, we miss them too. And one of these days, we'll be back home where we belong.

The weather is the same now as when you were here; sun, rain, sun, rain, and it's cool. Now that I have some clothes, I hope it gets warmer! Enough rain!

My rechaud (stove) is smelly, smoky, and messy. But it's brought some variation to my meals. I have pasta, rice with veggies, sardines, corn, and peanut butter and jelly (my favorite). If only I had soft, cheap white bread! The kosher canteen was messed up again, so I won't have any tuna or meat for the next three weeks. But maybe I'll be out soon. Every day is one closer to our liberation.

I felt something yesterday that I felt last week also. If I feel it again, I think it'll be safe to say that it's the baby, but it may just be indigestion! We're doing well and my spirits are pretty high, especially considering the circumstances. The girls here all have friends who've been liberated in the last week or will be in the coming week, so there's a good mood even among us who are in the dark about our sentences.

They tell me my French is getting better, but the language barrier is still there, especially when I want it there! Talking to the rabbi is so funny because I say a sentence in three languages, but he understands despite my English/French/Hebrew speech. Now I'm listening to Yiddish on the Jewish radio station, which usually is all in French and plays a variety of weird music. It often mentions Israel, but that's all I understand.

So Dad, what do you think of Israel's new prime minister? Is he good or not? Mom, how are the eyes? I think by now you had the surgery. I hope it went well and your recovery is going well. No lifting!! Just rest.

Oh, my kallah teacher had a boy over the long weekend. Mazal tov. So did a friend of mine, but in the previous week. With G-d's help, we should all share many more simchahs. The little boy that I wrote about that was so sick is in the hospital again, so keep those Tehillim going.

My friend Tamara is taking care of my KitchenAid for me and making challah as a segulah that we should come home soon! So all of our heartfelt prayers should be answered soon!

Well, hopefully the next few days will bring some answers. That's all over here. We love you and miss you lots and are waiting anxiously to come home.

Love,
Your daughter and the baby

She had torn up her pillow to make it more comfortable. When asked why in French by the angry guard, and she was afraid of possible consequences, she pretended not to understand his question. Having a language barrier, when needed, could come in handy. The guard finally left in frustration.

Time... Sometimes it stands still and sometimes it moves too fast. Her feared fellow inmates were now "the girls," white bread a longing, and freedom a dream.

29
Life Proceeds Even While It Stands Still

Dear Mom and Dad:

I just got two letters and a buffalo postcard. Thanks for sending more clothes. I should receive them soon. I guess your package will arrive this time and hopefully before the rabbi's next visit on Tuesday, and he'll bring them with.

The lawyers came this morning and I'm sure they'll tell you all about the visit and lack of news. I guess G-d has a plan and we'll just use the next month to daven and grow.

Well, it's lunchtime, so I'm going to eat. I made pasta salad with tomatoes, garlic, and avocado, salt, and of course pasta and a petit-suisse thing. It's somewhere between cream cheese and sour cream. I had it with whole wheat bread and butter. Yum!

Oh, I'm getting a powwow today! I guess with Betty. I'll write more later, but I better eat. I have one hour and you know how slow I am!

Well, powwow was very nice. Betty seems to know as much about the case as I do!! It's nice to have visitors that I'm not attached to. It's a nice break from routine and doesn't cause any emotional side effects. Aaron, our closest friend, will be coming to France soon, but only for a few days.

I've been thinking about the near future. It sounds hopeful that I may be able to leave prison on bail at the end of July/beginning of August (that's my impression from the lawyer). Maybe I'll be able to come and meet you for the Burtons' wedding, depending on where the case is at. Maybe go back to France or come home until the baby is born and a bit after. In all this, I hope Daniel will be with me. If not earlier, then at least in time for the baby.

I'd like to stay with you with the baby for at least one month. I think that's the minimum for health reasons for both the baby and me, and then hopefully relocate with my hubby and baby.

Now this "plan" has many holes because at the moment we're both in France locked up. But that is the idea. So with that plan, our old apartment is useless until January. And that only would be used if we return. Besides, as soon as we can, we're going to find a different apartment. My sentimental desire to go back to my home is nowhere as important as the facts. We have no money and we're not being a source of income now, but OUTcome. So if we plan on setting up our life again, every penny counts. So the money that's going to the landlord is a big waste.

That was the idea before and it has been strengthened by the news from the lawyers today. I don't think people realize that we won't be in that home till at least January, if not later. So that means April, May, June, July, August, September, October, November, December. We're paying $850/month for storage and to keep the apartment, so it won't offend anyone.

Now that doesn't make sense. Our friends know, because we're writing to them, that we appreciate their friendship and will be home as soon as we can. They're already waiting to pack our apartment, which hopefully won't be a problem even though they're not family.

I don't appreciate strangers cleaning, clearing out, and possibly snooping through our apartment without our permission. I've written this to Daniel and he agrees. All that money that is going to pay rent can go either in a bank for when we return or to pay the expenses now.

Health insurance is an issue too. But an apartment isn't as vital. We'll be able to find something. If we need to stay temporarily somewhere I don't think that will be a problem. As soon as we can, we need to get jobs to start making some money. Just keep your eye out for me to see how much I could charge for a wash/style at home. And maybe I could work at the school part time. We'll have to see how I'll be feeling, of course. For the month or two after the baby, sheitels may be all I'll be up to.

Daniel may still have his old job, which would be fantastic! But then again, I don't know how long that guy is willing to wait for him. So...I thought of doing babysitting once I'm back and settled. There will be a number of births this summer/fall, so perhaps me and another girl would do babysitting. We can then stay home with our babies and make a bit of money! Don't people realize that the $850/month would be better put towards our living expenses when we get home and not into rent?

Of our furniture, the only thing I'd like to keep is the beds. The others we can get cheap replacements of, but our beds are good, and since we'll be starting out again, this time with no money, we can't make investments in our furniture. The couches, tables, chairs, bureaus, dressers, etc. can all be sold, but we won't get close to what they're worth.

Well, enough complaining. So now you have my newest, dearest ideas on the future. Let me know what you think of all of it.

The lawyer said Aaron is coming and I'll ask his opinion. He's a smart guy, and it seems that others think so too. I'll try to get him to pass our messages on.

So Mom, I guess your surgery wasn't last week since you were just back and maybe it was this week, so I'll keep you in my Tehillim. Let me know how you're doing, and I hope the heat isn't too bad for you, Pops.

Please send love to Josh. Tell him the picture he sent is very nice. I keep it close to my bed with a few other guaranteed smile makers. This way, I see them right when I get up. What's doing with his apartment? Does he want to stay and move to my area for a while and check it out? I know a nice two-bedroom apartment on a dead-end street!

Well, time for my nap. I'll send this out tonight so you should get it by next Wednesday/Thursday.

Lots of love, kisses, and hugs too!
Mom and Baby

It took us three days to drive back home from the bar mitzvah and engagement party. At each stop, I looked for maternity clothes to send Miriam. I was slated to return to work after the summer. Life proceeds even while it stands still!

Her visitor, Betty, was a woman in France who knew a friend of Daniel's. Having heard about their situation from this mutual acquaintance, she befriended my children. Betty had been visiting my son-in-law, and I was grateful she would see my daughter.

It saddened me to read Miriam's unrealistic view of what would be allowed. It was wishful thinking, not accepting the reality of her situation, to think that she would be let out of the country on a promise to return. She was about to miss celebrations of family friends who were as close as family. That was probably too painful to accept at this point. It would acknowledge that this imprisonment was going to last a long time.

I could hear her frustration with each mention of "no news" from the lawyers and talk of delays. I could hear her anger at having her wishes and those of her husband disregarded about their apartment.

I noted her lack of focus caused by fear in her constant retelling the things said in the last letter. What amazed me most was her constant concern for us while she was in the middle of her own suffering. Where did she find the room?

30
Happy First Anniversary

The next letter arrived with a big blue heart penciled on the envelope, with the note, "This is blue 'cuz I miss you!!" Printed on the other corner were the words, "Baby pictures enclosed." With a bittersweet smile, I opened the envelope. The drawings of a child, my child. The blue heart brought joy and tears to my eyes. My baby was having a baby. She was only twenty-one, in prison, pregnant, and alone.

June 13

Dear Momma, Poppa, and Brother Bear, (sorry, I'm in a weird mood) —

Hiya gang! It's a beautiful day here in France, or at least what I can see of it. Shabbos was nice. My meals were full of song and the words of Torah you sent. Erev Shabbos, as usual, was tough. It's hard to prepare Shabbos just for yourself. It reminds me that I'm here in prison — alone — physically. But, thank G-d, I have all the pictures and cards and letters from you and all our friends to remind me that you're all with me in my heart.

As I get into the zemiros, and especially Shabbos afternoon when I learn Pirkei Avos with the baby, my mood improves. So overall Shabbos was nice. Also all the letters that I got on Shabbos morning was a big help. Since they're opened by the prison,[3] I get to read them too. I got a postcard from the Fines but with no return address, so say hi and thanks. Tell them that their daughter can have my address!

Please send the Burtons and Bubba Bella my condolences. I'm so sorry to hear the news. Thank G-d they were able to see him not that long ago and he shared in the simchah of the bar mitzvah. It's great that they have another celebration coming! With G-d's help, we should all share only simchahs!

Well, it seems like since you wrote, the apartment problem has (finally) been resolved. It has been rented as a furnished apartment to a newlywed couple with our furniture. So our stuff is gonna be packed up. Please utilize our friends who very much want to help and feel useful in packing. Our sefarim can be used by our friends rather than sit in boxes. They should be used in our merit! I wrote the same to everyone involved today and hopefully they'll listen— but you never know.

It seems Josh wrote Daniel an upsetting letter. From what I understand, Josh blames Daniel for this whole mess because he feels Daniel shouldn't have trusted his friend and should have done more to protect me. I'm not sure if Daniel's emotions made more of what Josh actually wrote. But I don't think that was helpful or nice. First, Daniel would never do anything to hurt me. Also, we are not emotionally strong enough now to receive upsetting, accusatory letters from our family.

Please tell Josh to be gentle, and if you have something negative to say, say it softly or even hold off until we're home. I know that the only

---

3. One is forbidden to tear (and thus open envelopes) on the Sabbath.

thing pulling me through the loneliness and extreme isolation are the letters of love and encouragement from family and friends. Daniel feels the same way. Please try to be understanding. If this is all unnecessary because Daniel read too much into Josh's letter, please forgive me.

Anyway, on a better note. I'll see the rabbi Tuesday, and he'll probably have your package, which I am looking forward to.

How are your eyes? I'm sending you the most recent echograph from May 4. I'll probably have another one in two or three weeks, and after Daniel, you'll get the pic too. Maybe I can get two pix. Well, this one, although a month old, is better than the first one. Scan 'em and then send 'em back! Maybe we'll just come pick 'em up!

Mom, your card was so nice! I'm glad you had fun shopping for the maternity stuff. Just wait, soon we'll shop for baby stuff together!!! I hope that you've gotten some sleep — both of you! I'll sing to the baby for you if you take a big zopiclone and sleep. You need your rest. Worrying all night helps no one! Least of all yourself. Please take care of yourself and your health. With G-d's help, soon I'll be there with you (maybe, please G-d, with Daniel) and there will be much excitement and you'll need to have energy! So rest and take care of yourself!

Dad, what's doing with your courses? The ones you're giving and are you taking any? You'll probably receive this Monday, the 21st, so happy anniversary on your daughter's wedding. It's our Hebrew anniversary.[4] Can you believe it's been a year! Wow.

The weather has improved, but is still very weird — nice and sunny then rain! Oh well, this is better than the three days of straight heat we had just after you left. It's better to be too cold than too hot. I have clothes, blankets (but it's not that cold). When it's hot, the heat goes nowhere.

Still no definite word from the kid, but I'll let you know. This (or

4. The English calendar is based on the solar year, which is 364¼ days, whereas the Hebrew calendar is based on the lunar year, which 354 and a fraction days. Therefore, the dates do not always coincide.

next week) is the time *I* should detect baby movements.
So…let's just be patient.

Lots of love, a few kisses, and hugs too,
Your kid and grandkid 2 B

The baby picture was an ultrasound. She had begged the doctor for a copy.

She told me later it often depended on the prison doctor's mood if she'd give you a copy. My daughter had so little control of her own life. Any request, hope, could be dashed, even an ultrasound picture of her baby.

Mail, of course, was opened by the prison and read. This was both outgoing and incoming. As always, she found the bright side. Had the prison not opened her mail, she would have to wait until after Shabbos to tear open the envelopes. Having the letters right next to her but not being able to read them would have been so painful for her.

My friend Rosy, whom we had just visited to celebrate the bar mitzvah of one son and the engagement of another, had suddenly lost her father. She had come to our city and stayed with me during the funeral and seven days of mourning. The timing was horrendous. I had just arrived home — finally — after a month in France, several days at her home sharing the celebrations, and then a three-day drive home.

The night before I had told my husband that I was going to bed and would probably not get up until all this was over. I was exhausted and very depressed. The next morning, we heard from Rosy. Her dad was in intensive care, and she was coming in. She got to the hospital too late to say good-bye. Reuben and I helped with the funeral and the mourning period as best we could, bringing food, trying to console. My rest was put on hold.

Later, when I praised my daughter for her strength and caring of others during her time of adversity, she asked me where I thought she had learned to act that way. She reminded me that Rosy had stayed with us for her shivah, "with exhausted you," she said.

Miriam was scared and in prison. My son reacted to her state in a letter he wrote to Daniel. Daniel, being in his own hell, fearful and alone, misinterpreted what Josh had said. It was such a laden time for us all, so full of fear and unknowing. Everyone's emotions were spilling over.

Her first anniversary had come and gone, with each in their separate prisons awaiting word on their future.

31
The French Angel

Dear Mom, Dad, and Josh:

Hi guys! It's 5:15 and today has been a busy day. After breakfast, the psychologist from one of the hospitals visited again and spoke with each of us. It's sort of lame, but it's required. Then I davened, and since today is Rosh Chodesh it was long. Then lunch. I had my fave (or one of my favorites, I guess I really like food)! Peanut butter and jelly with milk — not on cheap white bread, but on prison French bread. Oh well, it was good anyway. Then I had an orange and banana for dessert.

I was expecting to meet Tikva today, but no one announced a powwow. They usually tell you an hour before. Then at 1:30, they came to get me. Well, at least they didn't completely mess up. She's very nice! She said she brought clothing and money and will come next Monday, I should prepare laundry. She has a royal way. I don't know what it's called, maybe grace. When I came back at 3:00 my canteen came.

I received the letter from you that Dad typed on Sunday (the 6th), so it's still taking eight days for mail to get here. By now, I guess, the

111

shivah is over and Rosy is on her way home, so you will finally get time to rest. Please take advantage of it. With G-d's help, we will soon be able to come home and we will have much to do.

Not much else today. Daniel writes that his roomie fell into a depression, because his brother — his only helper — suffered a sort of nervous breakdown and became an alcoholic. He needs Daniel's friendship and encouragement even more now.

Well, like Tikva was assuring me, G-d has plans we may only one day learn about. We are all optimistic about the next meeting of the lawyer and Her Honor. I hope and pray it will bring us all good news.

I love you guys lots and soon we will see each other — maybe even take a Lamaze class!

Mom and kid

This letter came in an envelope with a pink heart on it, with the added scribbled note, "Sorry the letter is so short, but mail — even brief — is better than no news. So enjoy and more is coming."

Tikva was the angel I was destined to meet in France. A friend at home had given me her phone number and said I should contact her. Not waiting for me to call her, she called me in our rented room and insisted I let her help me. This was the beginning of an incredible friendship for me and an even deeper relationship for my daughter.

Tikva insisted we come to her home for meals and stay with them for Shabbos, and next time we came to France (if we had to come again, G-d forbid) stay with them. She and her family were supportive and caring beyond words.

Tikva signed up to visit my daughter, though having never met her; she took her laundry and later took her into her home. Her family helped me welcome our new grandchild and opened their home and their heart to our family. I am humbled and proud by my association with her and her family. Her husband supported her totally in her concern and caring for us and gave us his own uplifting support. They have two wonderful daughters, who later would often give us their bedroom and joyfully shared their home and parents.

Tikva came to feel more like a sister to my daughter than a friend. She called me after each visit and updated me. This stranger, this angel.

32

A Finger in the Dike

Dear Mom, Dad, and Bro:

Hi guys. So Mom, how was your surgery? I hope you are recovering well, and by the time you get this, you are feeling much better. Please keep me up-to-date with your recovery progress.

It's 9:00 p.m. and today was a beautiful day, enough cloud to cool and enough sun to enjoy. But now, with no breeze, it's a bit stuffy in my room. I drank a lot today. I guess the heat makes you thirsty, eh?

This morning I got a letter from you guys and Dad explained to me about Josh's letter and Daniel's response. I asked Daniel to send me the letter so I could see what Josh said. I don't think he meant to offend. Maybe as a more objective party (sort of), I can explain the feelings to Daniel. When Daniel told me his feelings about the letter, I was surprised, and I told him that he should try to see if he read too much into the letter.

He was very upset, though, which explains his response to Josh, through the lawyer. That doesn't mean it's right. What it seems to me is that we

114

have a miscommunication and two insulted guys. So I asked Daniel to write my bro and ask him what he meant and explain his feelings to him, and I hope both of them can be open with their emotions about this. I would be so upset if their relationship ended over this.

Well, with other news, I'm very happy to hear that our friends and family think highly of us. I know I'd agree with what they say about you. I always was comforted in knowing what wonderful parents I have and they would always try to help me, as best they can, for me to be the best I could. And it seems your good intentions have also been felt by others whose lives you've affected. So please feel good about yourselves — you deserve it! Dad, thank G-d, I can handle the issues you are discussing with me in your letters. If anything comes up that I can't, I'll either try harder or let you know. Thank G-d, this has been a big growing process for me. From what Daniel writes to me, I feel he's also grown a lot.

Could you make me return address labels? I hate writing my return address here. But if you do, copy the address I use as the return on this letter.

I got a note from the lawyer that Aaron will, please G-d, arrive by this week to see us. I think he's going to come on Friday. The rabbi told me to write to request a visit on Friday instead of Saturday. I also asked for an hour. We'll see what happens.

Okay. Lailah tov. I'll speak to you more tomorrow. Love you! Shluffy good.

Hi! It's 4:30 Thursday (the 17th) and I got a letter from the lawyer that said my date (with the judge) is confirmed! So something will soon be decided. With G-d's help, it will be good.

We had a concert today — mostly classical: eight violins, two small bass, and one large bass (not prisoners). It was beautiful. And then some of the prisoners who take dance did a Moroccan dance and an African dance, and a rap dance. It was all very nice. I think there's another one tomorrow. It's the Music Fest in France now, so some nice *people offer to come to us here.*

Two girls are leaving on Saturday, so the pregnant are just me and two others. There are still six moms with little ones. One is in the middle of requesting an exit. It's good to see people going. Keeps you positive.

Well, that's all. I think the baby enjoyed the music. I'm not 100%, but I think s/he was dancing! Love from us both!

By now, I had gone through my third surgery on my eye. Another surgery was pending. My son-in-law, offended, sensitive, and in pain, had told my son that if all he had were accusations, he should not bother to write. This misunderstanding was escalating in a bad way. I had read the offending letter. I thought it had been quite supportive and encouraging. I wasn't sure how it had caused such hurt feelings. Even a benign message becomes malignant upon entering the prison walls.

Communication in prison was allowed by letter only. This, compounded by a two-week delay (one week until the mail arrived and one week until it returned), was wreaking havoc on relationships. My daughter, always the peacemaker, was determined to do just that — make peace between her brother and her husband. She was desperate for them to remain friends.

A date with the judge. Finally! But this was not the trial. It just meant the first judge, the investigating judge, had finished her research. There would be other judges who decided their fate. But this one was important. Her recommendations often influenced the other judges. She could also decide that there was no case at all and let them go. Another option open to her was to let them out, on a bail-like system, to a family in France who would take responsibility for them.

Over two months had passed and it would be at least another month before this judge would see them. Miriam and Daniel's future was literally in her hands for now. Meanwhile, they would spend the summer in the hot prisons.

We had been asked to get reference letters for our family and daughter. These would be passed on to the judge and hopefully would help her see that they were not drug dealers. We needed to collect as many as we could and have them faxed within twenty-four hours. Letters were to be from teachers and colleagues, friends and professionals who knew us and our daughter.

Getting the letters was easy. Asking for them, retelling the story over and over, was excruciating. We had decided early on not to say anything of the arrest except to a very small circle of close friends (three couples whom we could trust with confidences). Even though this meant limiting support for ourselves, it was a simple choice. We hoped our kids could come back to at least one place where people didn't know their story, where they could resume a normal life without people asking inappropriate questions.

Meanwhile, on the east coast, their story was running wild. What people didn't know, they made up and passed on. All versions were accepted as absolute truth. A friend, not realizing she was talking about my kids, told me that New York was buzzing with the story of this young couple who had gone to Amsterdam to trade diamonds for drugs and had been arrested. The girl had her baby in prison. The baby had been apprehended and placed in care!

A prominent speaker told the "true" story of a young couple who had been driven by need to theft. Giving enough details to identify my children but telling a story that was far from the truth, he painted a picture, though false, that could never be recanted.

I believed the saying, "In your mouth, you're the master. Out of your mouth, you're the slave." Until this was over, until Daniel and Miriam decided whether to go public or not, I would try desperately to keep them the master of the tale when so many people were making them the slaves. But it was like putting my finger in the proverbial dike, oftentimes with desperation and panic.

"How are you?" came a call from an old friend in New York.

"Fine!" The answer was so automatic these days. The hard part was keeping the depression out of my voice.

"I know," she said in a flat voice.

I struggled to stay calm, the panic rising. My dike was falling. "Know what?"

"I know your kids are in prison. I heard today."

"And what is it you heard?"

"Look," she said, "I decided, as the principal, to accompany one of my classes on a trip. The teachers, some mothers, and the school secretary came along. We were just chatting. The school secretary was telling us about this reference letter she had typed and faxed for the Hebrew principal yesterday. I know."

The water flooded over my dike and began to drown me. A feeling of helplessness and severe depression welled up in me. To this secretary, it was just a story; a good story for gossip and speculation. For me it was another weight added to a drowning person, making recovery even harder. My depression turned to rage.

"If it were my secretary, she'd be fired," I said angrily.

"She means well," came the reply. "She didn't know I'd know the people she was talking about when she mentioned their names."

I called our friend, the principal who had written the letter she had typed. He had lived in our community during my daughter's elementary education and served as her teacher many times. He was also a parent of her friends and a friend of ours. He too could not see that this breach of confidentiality deserved consequences. After all, she was a nice woman. He could not understand the harm that it had caused.

I had always been respectful and careful of confidences and demanded confidentiality of those who worked for me. Even so, the concept of privacy took on new importance for me now. I wondered, amazed, how people could treat other people's lives so very lightly.

Miriam and Daniel's good friend was traveling to France. The man who had located them, found and retained the lawyer, and helped us constantly throughout this mess was going to see them. To this day, I often wonder what we would have done without him. He was so young, but so smart and streetwise, savvy beyond his years in dealing with people and politics.

Obsessed with freeing them, he took constant abuse from people who wanted information and gossip that he refused to give. He got constant criticism from those who "knew better," though they knew nothing. He was yelled at by people who "deserved to know" because they "were friends" or "had known them when..." or had "prayed for them" and therefore felt "entitled" to information.

I was amazed at this man's strength and his wife's constant support. We were thirty years older, but he kept us focused and on task. He directed all the moves. We trusted him implicitly, followed his direction without question, and felt safe in his plan. He was obsessed and selfless in his goal of freeing them. He is the kind of person everyone would relish as a friend and fear as an enemy; an angel, a caring, giving human being, hiding in a rough exterior. He and his wife were our oasis and our kids' lifeline.

33

Bubbles and Bubby

Dear Mom, Dad, and Josh:

Hi guys! How's everything at home? I got a card from Mom on Friday and a postcard and a letter from Dad on Shabbos. The pix you sent with the letter were great! So Pops, as to the questions in your letter — the clothes are from Gertrude. I assume I'll get Mom's this week from the rav. How was last Shabbos with the Burton family? Quite a full house — I hope Mommy and Daddy didn't work too hard! Mom's got to rest that eye!

As you will see soon in one of the recent letters to you, it contains a letter to Bubby! I'm expecting Tikva tomorrow and I prepared some laundry for her. She also offered to do dry cleaning, but I think I'll hold off on that. I feel funny giving her any laundry!

I've decided that those "bubbles" I've been occasionally feeling are in fact the baby. They occur randomly, but last week we had a classical music concert. At this concert I had a bunch of them! Since then, I get one or two every now and then. Today is twenty weeks, so it's right on time, according to the books.

I moved rooms today, from 7 to 4. It's not any different, except it's a mirror image of the old one. The address info is all the same.

Two girls went home on Shabbos. One has an infant and the other's got one on the way. Shabbos was nice.

I read the divrei Torah you sent, one Friday night and the other one Shabbos day. Thank you and please send more. I got two skirts from Rachel, but they took one away because it's blue. I think I'm pretty well clothed for the time being. Hopefully we'll soon be seeing each other. It's a month till the next "big day," when hopefully we'll know something definite.

Oh, supper's here and I'm gonna leave room for tomorrow in case I get any news to share. Love ya. Good night.

P.S. The "bubbles" have been the baby kicks and moving around and s/he is doing it more now. Still occasional and not often, but enough that I realize what it is!

Good morning. It's Monday. I got a postcard and letter from you guys. The letter also had Mom's handwritten one signed "Bubby." I thought before I read it that it was a note from Bubby! Then I read it and saw it's you! So you got me this time!

To answer your letter: Pas and chalav Yisrael are just two items on our list of improvements. You'll be happy to know it also includes being careful not to speak lashon hara and "Those People" mitzvos, as well as some more "how to treat your fellow man" mitzvos. This is just one or two that are part of the improved package. The other kosher mitzvos are not difficult to do in most places and we may as well get extra points. We're looking for all ways to improve ourselves, so this is just a piece of our thinking.

Thanks for Bubby's zip code. I hope she's not running around with a pair of scissors looking for that guy and his tzitzis! I've decided that maybe he was also just a dummy here. It's a comfort to let go of my bad feelings towards him.

The job situation sounds decent and, depending on our future, may be useful. Thank you for your support — emotionally, physically, and financially. I can't wait to get Josh's letter. And I, of course, will take extra precautions with regard to my family's safety.

I got Rachel's stuff and I'm all set for clothes. This Tuesday, the rabbi comes and will bring your package too, I hope, and I'll have a good supply. I'm glad you're losing weight, Mom. It's good for your health, which is very important! I hope your eye(s) are seeing well! And the cold is gone. All is good and the baby has definitely been kicking — waiting to see you.

Your daughter and the baby

Being dependent was not her strong suit. To have a stranger/new friend do your laundry leaves you embarrassed and humbled and immensely grateful.

They had taken on resolutions of self-improvement. They would only eat milk and bread that had been prepared in a more stringently kosher manner. They had also taken on a commitment against gossip (having understood firsthand its extreme pain). "Those People" commandments were those relating to treatment of parents. For her bas mitzvah, Miriam had learned *Sefer HaChinuch*, and since then had jokingly referred to all obligations required of children to parents as "Those People" obligations. They had also decided to improve in regard to man's obligation to his fellow man. All this was positive, whatever the initial motivation.

In one month we'd know. The days of waiting that had turned into weeks and months. Finally, after months of anxiety, the judge would be ready to report. But the French system is different from ours. The lawyer would go to the judge's office at the set time. Perhaps he would see her, perhaps not. She was busy. Many people were given the same appointment. You had to wait in her office until called. It could take days or longer.

We wrote daily. We wrote about the weather, community events, anything that would fill the page. We knew just receiving a letter was the hope, the smile. The content was secondary. Miriam could have written nursery rhymes or repeated herself hundreds of times — I still would have treasured each letter. The letters that passed between us were the way we held hands across the miles.

34
Strange Visitors

Dear Mom, Dad, and Josh:

Hi family. How is everyone? I hope you are getting proper rest, and especially Mom. Got to get those eyes working well so you can read lots to the baby!! I got a nice card and letter from you guys today, along with many more from friends. Wow, our community sure is great. I always thought so! I hope we will soon be able to reestablish our home there and raise our kid(s) there. For now, France, then your house, then back to our home. But how much time in each place is still unknown!

Yesterday, Tikva came and took some laundry and gave me two books and a catalog (ArtScroll) to tell her what to order. I really like her! The clothing she gave me last time smells so nice. The two outfits she gave me are very nice and comfy. One is lavender. I even got a few compliments! Maybe I'll wear it to see the judge! I want to check with the lawyer, before I go, about everything. What should I wear, say, do, etc. I'm sure he'll tell me.

Anyway, I'm glad Daniel wrote to Josh. I hope they clear things up. We'll see what we'll do about living quarters when we get to your home. I would like to get back to my home as soon as it's safe, so we'll see. But time in your home will be great, whether it's one month or three! I know you guys want us as much as you can get us and that feels good!

Rabbi K. has been sending us postcards and might give the chaplain tapes or books for us. That means buying a tape player, so I may just save the tapes for home. How did things go with the VON? How is Josh?

Oh, Tikva said Mom might come again, will it be with Josh? Wait till the hearing before you do anything. Maybe I'll be coming home. They just brought me another postcard from Rabbi K. He said he gave tapes and books to some rabbi from France who was at his house, and this rabbi will give them to our chaplain for me and Daniel. That's so nice! I guess the chaplain is coming on Friday this week, and he'll bring the clothes you sent and maybe the books if he has them.

Well, that's all for today. Oh, we got a new lady. She's in her ninth month! She was busy today "checking in," so we'll all meet her tomorrow. So now there are four of us who are pregnant. One of the moms sent her son to the dad for two weeks. It's nice that they do that. It gives them both a break and lets the dad be involved, too. Okay, I'll write more tomorrow. Love you guys lots!

Hiya. I got two letters from you today, and a visit from two ladies Rabbi K. sent. Josh, I hope you got Daniel's letter and the two of you can sort out this mess. I think the communication was messed up. The two women who visited asked what they could do to help, etc., and casually asked about Daniel, the lawyer, the case. I said nothing about that stuff of course, but said they could bring books and visit Daniel too. I'm in a rush to get this out to you 'cuz they're bringing dinner soon and that's when the mail last goes out. Thanks for the excerpt from Rabbi Twersky's book. It's very good, like his other work.

The mail is very messed up. I got four letters from Daniel today, from the 16th, 17th, 20th, and 21st, but yesterday got one from the 18th and 20th also. So there's something kookoo! I guess they also get to you out of order. Oh, about food, I'm, thank G-d, eating well. Lots of yogurt, veggies, fruit, rice, pasta, sardines, corn, and milk, and with the kosher canteen, I get tuna and meat and hot dog — type things, so the nutrients are there. The only thing I'm missing is cheese.

Anyway, gotta hurry up. I love you lots and the little kicking grandkid-to-be does too!

Love,
Your daughter and baby

There was no certainty they would get out. Just hope. Hope was what we lived on...

Tikva had sized up my daughter well. Sensing her reluctance to inconvenience others, even in these dire circumstances, Tikva told my daughter it was my request that she purchase whatever the mom-to-be needed and I'd reimburse her. She put money in Miriam's account at the prison, saying it was from us. I didn't know about this until much later. By then, my debit account with this family could not be repaid in money. Their generosity to me, my daughter, my family; their responsiveness to every perceived need went far in restoring my faith in people at a time when it was being heavily tested. Tikva and her family gave me a model to strive for — to be as human to others as they had been to us.

Visitors sent by others — people she did not know — came to see Miriam. She wished the person who had sent them to visit her had told her they were coming. How often during her months of imprisonment would she be reduced to fear because of people's good intentions? The good intentions were real, but so was the fear, which was tangible and all consuming. And so she feared these ladies.

They said they had been sent by Rabbi K., but were they? He hadn't said anything in his weekly letters. Why not? They asked questions about her case. She panicked. Daniel and Miriam had already been set up once — they'd had no idea they were carrying drugs. Were these women good Samaritans or people sent to gather information? Miriam was in a prison cell twenty out of twenty-four hours a day with nothing but her imagination for company. There was a drug gang out there, something to be really afraid of. She didn't know who to trust and who to fear, so she feared everyone she didn't know. Fear was her only reality.

And still the clothes I sent had not arrived.

Letters were a gift, a lifeline to her. Whenever anyone asked what they could do, we told them to write, send cards, and be positive.

The constant rambling in her letters from topic to topic and back again, her constant repetition of information just reinforced for me the depth of her fear. Her need to be comforted by and connected to us was screaming through the artificial calmness of the words in her letters.

My husband had gotten a terrible infection and was on an intravenous monitored by the VON (Victorian Order of Nurses). My mother wasn't well. The implanted lens in my eye had slipped for the second time, requiring another surgery. Life doesn't stop just because you're in pain and feel you can't cope with another thing. Life goes on, expecting you to cope — and somehow, you do.

35
Human Life Preservers

Dear Mom, Dad, and Josh,

Hi guys. It's suppertime and I'm boiling water for rice. I fried tomato and green pepper already and am just waiting for the water to bubble. I'm also making some falafel patties. But they have to wait for the fire to be free.

No new info today. I got a nice letter from Rebbetzin J. and also Rebbetzin L., but hers was very short. Today was a beautiful day. I stayed out in the p.m. for two and a half hours. I spent half of it in the shade, though, 'cuz there were no clouds at all. A great day for the beach!

I got another card from Rabbi K. Some ladies came to visit me; I may have told you this in the last letter. I forget. Well, in case I didn't, I'll briefly tell you. They were awkward and me, too. Total strangers, but it was okay. Since I didn't know them, I gave no info about the case when they casually asked if there was any news.

My kosher canteen hasn't arrived yet. It was late last time also, so when I see the chaplain tomorrow, I'll ask him to check into it. Oh, water's ready — hang on! Okay. I'm gonna clean up a bit now, and prepare my candles for Shabbos. I'll speak to you more tomorrow.

Oh, did you get the letter for Bubby? Is it good? If so, send it please and then of course, you can talk about the baby and she can write to me. Mom, how's the vision? I hope you're healing well. And Dad, I'm so sorry I forgot Father's Day. I guess it wasn't on my calendar. Do they have these things in France? Well, when we get home, we'll have a special Father's/Mother's Day celebration, Mom'll tell you that I forgot her day, too. So much celebration when I get home! Till tomorrow! I love ya guys lots — always remember that and that we're doing well, thank G-d.

Hi guys! It's your anniversary! I hope you're having a happy one! I wish so much that we could be with you guys and make a nice party with you. I guess that will also have to wait. It's 10:20 and I'm in the "playroom." The mail didn't come yet, so no news to report.

Another mom and baby are leaving. She got "provisoir," the same type of thing I hope for. The nun will be back in a week. I hope her vacation was good. Baby just kicked — to wish you guys a happy anniversary! It's nice to have the assurance of feeling the baby now.

Well, I'm gonna "read" some French pregnancy magazines till they bring our mail, then I'll write some more. Hopefully I'll see the chaplain today and that's always good. I think he'll bring the clothes you sent. I'm so excited to see them! Thank you for them. I hope that we can get together for baby clothes — won't that be fun! Everything in G-d's time. Okay, till later.

Mail and my kosher food came. Yippee. I'm gonna read the mail and let you know what's doing.

Love ya!

I got two letters from Daniel. He sounds good, thank G-d. One from Betty because she couldn't come this week because those ladies (whose names they left for me in the mail and I got today) came. I'm gonna give their names to the lawyer to check out and the chaplain so he can be in contact with them. They want to give the chaplain food and books for me.

Anyway, they want to speak with Betty and Tikva about coordinating visits. I can get only one a day, two per week, but three people can come together. I like Tikva alone. I feel very comfy with her. She's a very special lady. I asked her to call you today to wish you a happy anniversary. I hope she remembers. She probably will. She's so nice.

Oh, I also got a letter from Rabbi B. It's nice and short. Wishes us well and his thoughts and prayers are with us and then asks what it's like here. He gives an update of his family. Naomi is driving! Wow, everyone is growing up. Well, I guess if I'm having a baby, she must be old enough to drive! He says, "Tough times don't last. Tough people do!" He's had his share to know!

Well, I just finished lunch, leftovers from last night. I slept very well, from 9:30 till 7:00. Unfortunately, I did not daven maariv!

So August 30 (please G-d) seems to be when Rita and Jordan become Mr. and Mrs. I hope to meet her before the wedding. Well, at least I hope to be at the wedding. Gosh, dancing will be a bit different with the baby being so big by then. I'll have to borrow something to wear! That will be an exciting wedding. Bella looks good. How is she doing now? Send her my love. How's Avi doing with work and moving and his health? And Richard, the newest member of the family, looks good too. Did you tell him he's gonna be an "uncle"? He's a nice guy. Is he gonna go with you to Jordan's wedding?

The pix are really nice, except everyone has crazy red eyes! Avi and Danny look like bodyguards. That looks like a cool tie, Dad. Is it new? And is the fluorescent green thing a new fashion statement or just a bag? *You guys look great!*

With G-d's help, soon I'll see you and we'll be home!! Till then, we're with you in every way but body! Happy to hear Mom's healing well!

Love ya guys very much,
Your daughter and baby to be

She had written my mother, but wanted to make sure it wasn't in any way provocative or painful. I would be the editor. My mother missed them terribly, and at eighty-nine could not understand how the authorities were still holding them. After all, the guy who sent them said he had tricked them and that they had no idea they were carrying drugs. Why wouldn't the police just believe him and let them go already?

I had had my third eye surgery. The two previous to this one had each failed unexpectedly. The results were good for a few weeks and then suddenly went rapidly downhill. It seemed another saga without end. Everything in my life was on hold. Huge open parentheses were dotting the story of my life, and I was waiting for The Ultimate Author to say "close parentheses."

Miriam had hoped to be at my friend's son's wedding. He was like a brother to her — as were all his siblings. His parents were a second set of parents to her, as we were to their children. When this first happened, the family had offered to help in any way they could. Their oldest son, a lawyer, offered to go to France, if it would help. Stan, the father, offered to come and stay with my husband while I was in France. An incredible offer from a man who never even takes a vacation from work. Rosy, dear Rosy, called several times a week. Just being there, holding my hand.

As I get older and go through more adversity, I seem to have an ever-decreasing circle of good friends. But those who stay are platinum!

My friend, Suzanne, to whom I confided early on, was there with her constant cards and encouragement. She'd drop by to get me out of the house, and sometimes planned things just to get me out of bed, when depression became too great. She never intruded or asked questions. She just listened and was there for me, like a life preserver to a drowning person.

Richard was an orderly we had hired to accompany and help my husband when we traveled. He had been with us for my daughter's engagement party and wedding and accompanied us now whenever we had to make some kind of trip. He had become more of a family member than an employee. He was more helpful and supportive than most of the people whom I had once called "friend."

William and Alice and Adrian and Anna were ever present with supportive vigil and help. We chose Chaya and Zucia for advice in matters we were too involved in to see clearly. Eppy and Moyo, though far away, were always there for anything we asked. Rochel called long distance every Friday, "just to say hi." Our friends Chaim and Pearl sent poetry, candy, and prayers. These are people who gave us air to breathe. I doubt that they even know how important their support was.

36
"Happy Wedding Birthday"

Happy Happy Happy Anniversary!

Wow, guys — it's a special day and I'm celebrating along with you! No distance can keep us apart. I am with you as you are with all of us, always!

I could not believe my eyes. The fax machine kept going and I stood there, unable to move. Tears streamed down my face. How did she do it? How could she even remember with all that was going on? Yet here it was. An anniversary greeting sent and delivered on our anniversary. It continued...

For a quick update! Baby is kicking nicely, a great feeling and reassurance!

Thank G-d, I got my kosher canteen order today. I'm all set up till

133

the 6th of Av, and with G-d's help, won't need anymore canteens after that! I got a nice letter and pix from Rosy today! You guys look great! I can't wait to see you. I wish I could get a pic of me to send you.

From what I hear, Daniel is getting in really good shape, so he'll be my personal trainer after the baby is born, b'sha'ah tovah u'mutzlachas. I'm, thank G-d, doing very well. All that I am lacking is being with the people I love and, thank G-d, that is only temporarily and with G-d's help, will soon be over!

My blood pressure today was 9/5; low, so if you have any ideas how to pick it up a bit let me know. But mine is low usually, 'cuz I'm so chilled out. The weather has gotten beautiful, like summer at home. Dry, sunny! Good for a beach! Well, that's all.

I'll be seeing Betty on Monday and someone I don't know on Wednesday and Tikva on the following Monday. So I've got good messengers sending me smiles, love, and encouragement.

Tikva is such a doll. I asked her to call you today to wish you a happy anniversary. I hope she remembers from Monday. If not, at least you'll have this. I love you guys so much. Please send Josh my love! I can't wait to be with you guys.

Love ya lots!

Your daughter and grandkid to be

P.S. Two questions: How're your eyes? How is Bubby?

We called our former doctor, now retired, to get ideas for Miriam's low blood pressure.

In order to explain why Miriam's own doctor wasn't dealing with the problem, we had to tell him the whole story. As I told over the story, I noticed my eyes closed in pain and my voice was flat, guarded. In the telling, there was no hiding from reality and with reality came unbearable pain.

The doctor was wonderful, concerned and nonjudgmental. He gave us some advice and suggested that if she was home for the delivery, it should be regarded as high risk because of the lack of continuity of care. He would help us find a doctor for her just in case she would be able to deliver at home.

High-risk pregnancy. The words echoed in my head like a ping-pong ball. Each bounce brought with it more and more fear.

Tikva did call and wished us a "Happy Wedding Birthday!" I loved the translation as much as I loved the translator.

A few days later, a card arrived from Miriam. She said she hoped it wished us a happy anniversary. It was hard to know how to order cards from the canteen, as her French was limited. Limited, but growing, and she had no idea what the card said. I never did discover what the card really said. I never wanted to. To me, what it said was perfect.

37
Pennywise

Dear Mom, Dad, and Josh:

I got two postcards and Monday and Tuesday's letters today! I've still got Mom (a bit more than usual) in my prayers. I'm glad I know the surgery is tomorrow. I'll say some extra Tehillim.

Thank you for the potential baby names. I've got what to think about now! Thanks for the pics, they're great. And thank you so much for the two divrei Torah on Korach. I'll read them with the baby or to the baby on Shabbos. I saw the rabbi, he told me Aaron is coming this week. He'll see me on Friday. It will be very emotional to see him. I'll spend the next few days trying to get my thoughts and feelings into words! I got a beautiful note from Meshulem and a nice card from Suzanne. She was very cheerful and, as usual, a good smile-source. She's a good person!

It's lunchtime, so I'm gonna make some food! I'll write some more later. Love you guys lots!

Hi there. I'm back from promenade. It's a beautiful day! I spent

136

an hour outside. I wrote another letter to Bubby, and I enclosed it in this envelope. I want you to check if it needs any censoring. If you want, you can redo it as necessary. I'm going to nap now for about 40 minutes before supper. I think I'll have sardine salad with the cream cheese—type product.

I got some aerograms and I'm going to be using those to write to you guys, since it's only 5 francs, which includes paper and envelope, rather than my current method, which is 6 francs, plus paper, plus envelope. Even here we can find bargains! Well, not a bargain, but it's at least not wasting money.

Since I don't have much news, I'll send the aerograms whenever they get filled, every two or three days. But I hope you get them all. Keep up those Tehillim. G-d is putting them together and soon they'll outweigh the other side!

Lots of love, hugs, and kisses,
Your daughter and baby

Aaron was coming to see them. His visit gave Miriam a sense of well-being and security. Excitement at seeing him was an understatement.

Our friends wrote her notes to help keep her spirits up. It meant so much to us. A burden shared is easier to carry.

She was saving us 1 franc on a letter and the cost of paper. That was about 25 cents. She continued to think outward, worried about how this all was affecting others. She continued to amaze me and make me very, very proud of the person she was.

38
Tough Moments

Dearest Family (the bubby, the zaidy, and the uncle!):

Hi everyone. I got a note from Dad, a letter and a card from Mom on Shabbos morning. I was having a tough morning, so it was extra good to get your letters. I'm happy to see the ecrou # is right. I got letters you mailed on the 21st only five days later, so maybe they'll come quicker now. Still, the guards here checking them causes a delay, so who knows. At least we have the rabbi, baruch Hashem, and all my visitors who can keep in touch with you and give you timely reports.

Aaron came here Friday afternoon, looking real sharp! It was so great to see him. He told me Mom's surgery went well and I hope and pray the healing is good. Take it easy — treat yourself well! The joke you sent was a nice smile, as was the "while you weren't looking" poem, but different smiles! I got a letter from the lawyer, who says he'll come see us this week. Does that mean he has news, or is he just personally checking in? I guess I'll know by Friday.

The enlargement of the baby pictures is great. I think I might get new ones in the 23rd or 24th week of my pregnancy. I hope by now you're able to talk to Bubby about the baby. Please reassure her as best you can that we're healthy. Oh, maybe send a baby pic?

I'm not sure if we're getting money for the use of our furniture now that our apartment was rented furnished, but we should be!

I hope by now the situation with Josh and Daniel is on the mend. I read Josh's letter. Daniel sent it to me for a better understanding, and it was a very nicely stated but tough letter. So I see both sides. I think the way Josh put stuff was good, but I understand 100% where Daniel is now (as I'm there, too) and that now is a time for encouragement, not potches. So yes, we realize our mistake! We've both accepted what a poor judgment call it was and see that we need to be much less impulsive and more thoughtful in our decisions, like Josh was saying. But from Daniel to me and vice versa we can say it, but from family to give you an extra whack, now is not the time. We're so busy with the very big pain of being separated from each other. But the letter said some really nice things and Daniel saw that, too. So I hope the miscommunications got cleared up.

I forgot to ask the chaplain about the clothes on Friday, but I still haven't gotten them. I'm happy you like Daniel's letter. He's getting a bit of us in him! (You're not joking when you say that!) But it's good to be one of us!

There was a concert today. It turned out to be a choir. About 35–40 lawyers make up the choir and they go to prisons to bring sunshine into cloudy days. They sang two English songs: "Freedom" and "Happy Day," an Italian one and three French ones and also "Yerushalayim shel Zahav"! It was nice and the baby was kicking, so s/he hears the music and reacts. S/he is either dancing or saying "cut it out." But I like it, so I play music a lot. Okay. I'm gonna leave some room for tomorrow, then send this out! Love ya lots, guys!

Hi there! It's Monday, 3:30. I'm chilling out at promenade. It is actually a bit cool, but it's nice. I saw Betty. She, like Tikva, is a special person. After her visit with me, she's going to Daniel! She said they don't allow you to reschedule and she didn't want him to be without a visit. She offered for you to email her letters for me or Daniel and she'll mail them and they'll go quicker. Also she'll take letters we send to her and fax them to you. Do you want to do that? The mail within France is two-three days, so that would considerably speed things up. But it means they wouldn't be 100% private. I do think she can be trusted not to read them, but I wouldn't want to be able to read someone else's mail. It's very tempting. So maybe occasional stuff can go through her. I'll wait to hear what you say.

I got two cards and two letters from y'all today! One was an anniversary card! It was so nice. Thank you. I'm so happy to hear that you, baruch Hashem, are healing so well. Be gentle with yourself, though! I have a good supply of clothes (food, too!), but I hope we find your package. Also both Tikva and Betty are doing washes for me. I have a mystery guest on Wednesday! I'll let you know who! Oh, tell Aaron that if we don't get any money for the use of the furniture, he should ask about putting it in storage!

I'm out of room. I'll start another letter tomorrow. Love ya!

The need for sensitivity permeated everything. Josh's letter was written tough because that's who he is. I remember him working for hours on that letter. Trying to say what he wanted and not upset or offend. I remember him saying to me, and writing to Daniel, that a mistake is only a mistake when you do it twice. He felt strongly that Daniel and Miriam should not have agreed to take the bag. They should have realized something was "up" even when it was a good friend who asked. Josh had misinterpreted Daniel's bravado for smugness and was trying to help him "get it" and take responsibility. Daniel and Miriam, meanwhile, had more responsibility than they could take!

Depression was hovering around Miriam. She had been in prison almost three months, and the fear of having her baby in prison hung over her constantly.

Letters were her lifeline. There was a world out there with people she knew and cared about. It was normalcy. The life she had left and desperately wanted to resume.

We had the wrong *ecrou* number (whether that was her cell number or prison number, we never knew). Having the wrong number kept mail from her even longer than necessary.

We had had disagreements about how to handle things. We wanted to give the kids as much freedom as we could. Others wanted to control and protect. The differences in our approaches continued to cause a great rift.

Their goods had been removed from the apartment, but the furniture was to remain and be used by the new tenants, who had rented the place as a furnished apartment. Daniel and Miriam were not receiving any compensation for the use of the furniture and wanted it put in storage or sold. They asked us to facilitate that for them, causing more disagreement.

I discovered that their mail was being collected by their landlord. At the request of the person who had offered to forward their mail, it was opened and read to him over the phone. He then instructed the landlord what to send and what to destroy. I had always been very careful about respect for privacy and tried to instill that in my daughter. Having her mail scrutinized was not to Miriam's liking. At her request, I went to the post office and had their mail rerouted to them, unopened (until it got to the prison, of course).

Daniel and Miriam asked me to put their furniture in storage. When I spoke to the tenants, who were a lovely couple, they were shocked that Daniel and Miriam were not being reimbursed for the use of the furniture. They immediately offered to buy it. I told them I would ask my kids, as it was their decision, not mine.

Daniel and Miriam figured what they remembered having paid for it all and reduced the price by 20 percent for the few months of use, and it was sold. We placed the money in a bank account, where it would be to help them start over. It surprised me that listening to and implementing the instructions of our imprisoned children caused more problems for us — we were subsequently accused of pocketing the furniture money.

39
Pseudoparent

Dear Meshulem (aka Ta),

Thank you so much for your letter. I know that you haven't written because you're not a writer and I understand. Until now, I wasn't much of a letter writer, either. But now since it's my only way to communicate with those I love, I've become one.

So let me tell you a bit about life here. Each day is basically the same. We get woken up at about 7:30. They come to our door to empty our garbage cans and give us breakfast, hot water, and a tripack containing powdered milk, coffee, and sugar. Since I'm in the nursery, I also get a yogurt with the standard breakfast.

Then we're left till 9:00. At that time, we're welcome to go outside to the courtyard for an hour. At 10:00 we can go to a room with a TV, magazines, books, puzzles, etc. I usually go there and read my mail, while another lady watches music videos. Then at 11:00, we're escorted back to our rooms.

At 11:45 lunch comes, all treif, but we in the nursery get supplements of milk, yogurt, or some type of dairy, which is usually kosher. I have a stock of kosher foods as well as fresh products and canned goods, so I'm eating well.

Then sometime between 1:30 and 2:00, we again can go outside to a different courtyard. This one is mixed with all the first-timers and us nursery folk. They invite you back in at 3:00 and at 4:00, when it ends. I usually go in at 3:00 and try to nap a bit. I have trouble staying up till 11:00 for maariv otherwise.

Then at 5:30, supper comes. I usually heat up some food, make a salad, or invent some creative way to use corn, sardines, and falafel mix. I forgot to mention that I have a "stove" — a container/stand that holds combustible pastilles, which are meant as heaters — like to keep food warm during a smorgasbord. And on top of this, you can put a pot in which I've cooked rice, eggs, pasta, falafel, milk.

Actual cooking or boiling water uses many of the pastilles, so I've purchased a thermoplunger. It's a metal coil with a plug that boils water. I hope this proves to be a better method of heating the water. I'll get it on Tuesday. Supper is delivered with a "bon soir" (good night) from the "surveillantes," ladies in white lab coats who watch us and tend to our needs (occasionally). We don't usually have guards in uniform in the nursery.

After supper at 5:30 or 6:00, the door is closed for the night, and I entertain myself by preparing food for supper till about 7:00. Then I say minchah at a set time that I arrange with Daniel. Then I eat. At 9:00 I say the day's Tehillim plus the chapters for my mother, father, brother, Daniel, his parents, his sisters, and a sick boy. He's two years old and has leukemia. If you can add him to your prayers, I'll let you know if and when there is any news about him.

The Tehillim usually takes me 30-40 minutes and then I read or write until 11:00, then say maariv and Shema and go shluffy. Shabbos is difficult, but only emotionally. Thank G-d, I have encountered only a few problems, which with explanations (and patience), we ironed out.

Erev Shabbos is hard. Once I'm eating my Shabbos meal, my mood has generally improved. Again, during the day I sometimes get a bit blue, but my meals and even more so, learning Pirkei Avos with the baby cheers me up.

We get mail every day between 9:00 and 11:00, except on Sundays. It is one of the things that keeps me holding on so strong. That and the baby and the love and support from my family and friends, of which you are included as friend and as family. I'm sure you can see a difference. Everyone has family who is in the family category, but not in the friend category. A girlfriend of mine from New York is in the friend category, but not the family. You're one who is in both. I feel close to you as a family member — an unbreakable connection. I feel close to you as a friend, a chosen loved one. Thank G-d, I have many in each and a few in both. All have shown their support in this difficult time.

Also, on the positive side, this gives Daniel and me time to strengthen our own relationship with G-d, something which unfortunately had gotten stale over time (as is natural if there is no constant input). We had gotten into a comfortable place and "fell asleep." Well, we got our wakeup call loud and clear. Thank G-d, it was before the baby and all the responsibilities that come with being a parent. We've been given a timeout where all we can do is bond with G-d. So that is one of the great blessings we've gotten through this.

It's almost a year since our wedding. Tomorrow is our Hebrew anniversary, but our English one isn't until next Friday. Funny that my parents' anniversary is only a week before ours — plus thirty-three years, of course! I guess it's also an anniversary for you too. Your divorce was final about the same time as our wedding, wasn't it?

How are you doing? Are you interested in getting married again? How are the boys and your grandson? Do they call him Daniel? It's a nice name. How's your mother doing? Please send them all my love.

What's new in your life, or not new? I feel like we haven't spoken in a long time. Please continue to be a supportive family/friend to my parents. My father cherishes your relationship so much. You are indeed special to us. I hope your health's good. Please make sure it is! Take good care of yourself. With G-d's help, I will see you in the near future.

Love,

Your "daughter," Miriam

P.S. I know you have daughters-in-law now, but you didn't get any new daughters, did you?! Well, it's about 9:00 and time for Tehillim. Thank you for keeping me company this evening. I'm sorry I didn't write back last week when I got your letter, but I had run out of paper which arrived Thursday. With Shabbos and my visit from Aaron Friday, I was busy till today. So whenever you get a chance, just send a postcard.

Our friend, Meshulem, received the above letter from Miriam and promptly faxed it to us. He had been a pseudoparent when she was away at school. He was there with birthday gifts and rides to the airport before holidays. She was his "daughter" after his six boys, and he was the parent on call.

She had remembered that his divorce had been finalized on the day of her wedding. I remembered how she had spent time with him then, to encourage and support him, even though she was getting married a few hours later.

Prayers for the sick, prayers for the needy, for those in pain. After four long months in prison, Miriam's selflessness still astounded me. I hoped others were praying for her as she was for them.

40
Searching for Meaning

Dear Momma, Poppa, and Brother Bear:

Hi ya, how are y'all? Cow are you? Moo! Today was an exceptionally boring day. There was no mail. So I wrote a lot to people who I "owed" letters to. Oh, if you guys can check in with Daniel's grandma. I don't think she knows about us. She was having health problems. Thanks.

France is weird. All day, it was cloudy and dismal, now at 6:30, it's sunny? This whole country is backwards.

A friend of mine sent me a d'var Torah similar to one Dad sent about Megillas Rus. The commentary about Elimelech having to leave his home and comfort and easy observance because he was not all he could be. His "purity" of lineage only coming in the end from being in a place of impurity and his experience there. Kinda sounds maybe a bit like us? Our comfy "kadosh" life was not producing holiness, so we had to go into impurity — prison — for holiness to come forth. Well, that's how I heard it. Let me know what you think.

It's suppertime for me. I'm having my fave, peanut butter and jelly on French bread, too bad we can't get cheap ol' Wonder Bread. Yesterday I had hot dogs, Israeli-style, with hummus and tehina! Well, it's good and much better than the slop they give. Sunday's meal was RABBIT, yes, little bunny rabbit. Thank G-d we keep kosher. A few people said they ate it thinking it was chicken! No thank you!!

Well, tomorrow is my mystery guest! After I see whoever it is, I'll write you and finish this letter. I hope you're getting them. I think the aerograms go quicker because there's no way I can put anything forbidden in it. We'll see.

Good night for now. Remember I love you, miss you, hope to see you soon, and we're doing well.

Hi, wonderful family. It's Wednesday afternoon, 5:30. Supper and mail pickup is coming soon, so a quick lowdown on today. I got mail and labels from you. Thank you very much. My visit was from a Mrs. Kravetsky (whose hubby has seen Daniel twice). They're American and have lived here 14 years. He knows very little French. They're very nice people.

I also go to a patchwork class/activity. I'm making a mini decorative pillow! That's all for today. The lawyer wrote he would visit this week. Probably Friday. I'll let you know. Please send my love to Suzanne. Interesting ideas on videos, we'll see. Soon, Dad, you can hug Daniel and me! But the letters are like hugs for now! I'll write more in the next one, okay. I have two minutes. Yes, putting life back together will be a big job, but a special, worthwhile one we hope to do with joy. Mom, I hope the healing eye continues to do well.

Lots of love,
Miriam and Baby

The story of Ruth is read and studied on Shavuos by Jewish

communities around the world. In her community of one, Miriam did the same. Searching for meaning. Why me? Why this? If biblical characters needed to leave their homes in order to elevate their spirituality, how much more sense it made for her and Daniel to have a timeout (as she was fond of saying) to concentrate on their own ideals and elevate themselves. This view of events gave her solace and acceptance.

Mystery guest. Friend? Enemy? A visit to look forward to or fear? The unknown is frightening. The thought of being locked up with a stranger for half an hour, dodging questions, was so frightening. Were they there for her sake or part of this drug ring wanting information?

The visitor turned out to be a wonderful woman whose husband, Rabbi Kravetsky, had just begun to visit Daniel regularly. Daniel and the rabbi studied Torah together. He helped Daniel cope and, on bad days, raised his spirits. Rabbi Kravetsky answered practical questions of observance and got Daniel the religious books he asked for to fill his time constructively.

Videos. We had exchanged several letters on how to deal with this traumatic experience and help them turn the experience into something positive. I had suggested that they share their experience with high school and seminary students, warning them how easily you could be fooled even by trusted friends. We talked about making a video to that effect. Their other option was simply to remain anonymous and never look back.

As always, each letter talked of seeing us soon and being home. It had been so long, and still no word from the judge. How long would they have to wait in limbo before they could begin to deal with whatever their fate would be?

41

The Three Weeks Begin

Dear Mom, Dad, and Josh:

Hi, my special family.

Well, today is our first wedding anniversary on the English calendar and also Shivah Asar B'Tammuz.[5] This anniversary is mostly a "paper" one. All the beautiful cards from you and Daniel are already hanging up. Our celebration will be delayed this year. Not only are we apart but on a day like the Seventeenth of Tammuz, celebration is not really proper. With G-d's help, this day next year, we should all be celebrating in the Beis HaMikdash together with shalom and much, much simchah!

Daniel tells me that the Even HaShesiyah in Jerusalem is leaking water. He said many rabbanim feel it's another sign that Mashiach is coming to end the exile! Being here, in my little own exile, has really

---

5. As the English and Hebrew calendars do not always coincide, that year their English anniversary date fell out on the Hebrew calendar on the Seventeenth of Tammuz.

made me think. At home, the exile of our people from Israel doesn't feel too bad. But here, now, I have developed a real sense of that mourning for all we have lost since we lost the Temple. So many Jews have been lost to horrible troubles. Many, too many, are lost to assimilation — a quiet plague. We so badly need Hashem to send Mashiach and save us all. We are each suffering individually and, as a nation, we suffer together. So enough! We want Mashiach now.

I hope that Hashem sees the efforts that we all are making. Not only our family and friends, but the people here who only know us as fellow Jews! Maybe Hashem will respond, too, by saving us all. Not just by taking Daniel and me out of prison but by taking us all out of our own individual prisons. A complete redemption. Just imagine walking into the Beis HaMikdash and listening to the Levi'im! It's a dream yet, but it will soon come true. We must all make it happen!

I'm out of room, but have enough to send my love.

Your daughter and baby

The fast of the Seventeenth of Tammuz commemorates the breach by the Babylonians of the outer wall of Jerusalem in the time of the First Temple. It is the beginning of the Three Weeks of national mourning, which end on the Ninth of Av. That year, the Seventeenth of Tammuz coincided with their first anniversary. It was somehow appropriate. They had spent much of their first year of marriage apart and imprisoned.

Prison had taken Miriam out of her comfort zone. She was no longer in a Jewish neighborhood where everything she needed, from kosher food to religious books to ceremonial candles, was easily accessible. She was in exile.

42
A New Normal

Dear Family,

Shabbat shalom u'mevorach.

I hope you're getting my letters. I try to write each day now. I hope Mom's eye is healing as well as can be! Please continue to update me. So did you cool off yet, Dad? I'm sure the house at least is cool! Here, it's pretty mild, although the weather is crazy. We have rain, sun, wind, cloud, all in one hour!

Could you please get in touch with Rabbi Cohen, my former teacher? He's a special source of good things for me and I could use that as much as possible now. I also want to let him know about the baby. Have you spoken with Bubby yet? Did she get my letter? Please let her know how well we're doing. Please keep sending words of Torah, it's great!

That's all for today. Tomorrow is a big day. Perhaps the lawyer will come with a date for us to see the judge. Please pray it should happen.

Hi there. It's Friday, 12:30. I'm about to eat lunch — noodles, cheese, tomatoes, onion, garlic, all mixed together. Yum. But since I don't know when this letter will go out, I want to have it ready. No news from the lawyers yet. I guess no news is good news. I got an anniversary card from Rosy today and a beautiful card from you.

A psychologist from the court came with the interpreter to ask me questions. He asked about your job, age, Josh, my education level, my previous jobs, Daniel's age, jobs, and the case, basically how it occurred, my thoughts/philosophy on drugs, and my thoughts on my future. They also asked if this was a unique experience and what my religion felt about drugs. I told him the truth with as few words as possible. He says I'm "normal." The interpreter said it's nice to see me again. He said he'd see me soon. I'm going to write all this in detail to the lawyer.

Love ya lots. Have a super Shabbos. We'll see each other soon.

Miriam and Baby

Each letter seemed to repeat the previous one. Talk of weather, health, visits, anything normal. Anything that was not judges, dates, prison.

Rabbi Cohen was a teacher and guide Miriam had met while in high school. A special man, he was sensitive, caring, and always there for his students. I remember getting a call from him long after parent-teacher interviews. He apologized for not having called during the phone interview time. "We often forget to talk to the parents of our excellent students, especially when they live so far away, and that's not right."

He proceeded to tell me how highly he thought of my daughter, her ideals, her *middos*. I shared with him how she held him in awe and wanted to emulate his way of relating to others. As she matured, he had become her *posek* and mentor in whom she could confide and seek advice.

"Let Bubby know how well we're doing," she had said in her letter. The day before had been her anniversary. She was alone in her cell in a foreign country, but she wanted others not to be concerned.

I had taken a stress leave from work. I had begged confidentiality from human resources. They assured me of it. My principal had difficulty being left out of the loop. He began to call and leave me messages, asking about the nature of my illness and when I would return. He asked staff members to call on weekends to get the scoop. I screened our calls and didn't return most.

Having someone who spoke French with you could get you through quickly and with the least amount of aggravation. When Betty went to the Palace of Justice to apply for permission to visit Miriam and Daniel, the man behind them in line overheard the conversation. He was the interpreter assigned to the case. He would be present at every contact where a translator was needed. We saw this man quite often, and he went out of his way to put my daughter at ease and help her during these times.

Late that night we received a call from the lawyer. The judge would see them on July 19 and render an opinion, which would have great weight on the verdict. She would also decide whether or not Miriam could be released on bail. We had been told that Daniel would probably not get out on bail, but Miriam had a chance, as she faced lesser charges and was pregnant. Daniel insisted repeatedly that he wanted her freed. He even suggested taking on her sentence, whatever that would be. He just wanted her out!

July 19 fell during the Three Weeks, that period which represents the catch basin of catastrophe for Jews. We toyed with the idea of requesting a postponement of the judge's decision. But if we requested a postponement, who knew when it would take place. Everything in France closes in August, and the courts take a hiatus as well. Postponing could mean a delay of two, maybe three months.

We all discussed this, the lawyer, Aaron, and ourselves, but were unable to come to a conclusion. We decided to ask a *she'eilah*, and were told to let the procedure take place on the scheduled date. And so we left it in G-d's hands.

Fear and Forgetfulness

43

Dear Family,

I just mailed a letter, but I wanted to remind you to please get in touch with Rabbi Cohen ASAP. I would very much like to hear from him, especially now that we have a date. He has always been a special comfort and source of inspiration for me and now is a great time for both! Thanks.

I'll write more tomorrow. I hope there will be mail from you. Sometimes I get a few in one day and none the next. But since none came today, I kinda expect some tomorrow. The lawyer said he'd be by this week if he could. The chaplain, too. Love ya lots!

Well, it's Friday, 5:15. The chaplain didn't come today and neither did the lawyer. But I got a beautiful card and letter from you and a card from Rosy. I sent her a letter today.

When the psychologist from the court came with the interpreter to ask me a zillion questions, I was sort of nervous. It's been months and what happened is not as clear now. I don't remember too much about the little

155

details. He ended after 20 minutes. The interpreter said he'll see me on the 19th when we meet the judge. I guess he's my personal interpreter. Those questions seemed a bit strange for a psychologist to ask. I wrote it all in great detail to the lawyer and he'll let me know.

I'm surprised the chaplain didn't come. Oh well, perhaps Tuesday. I'd like to see him. I also look forward to any news he has from you! I guess we'll both have to wait till his next visit. I have to prepare wicks for my candles and somehow take a nap before Shabbos. As you know, I have a very hard time staying up till 11:00 for maariv.

Well, only two weeks (okay, 16 days) till our hearing! I hope everything goes well. It's very hard not to get my hopes up. I'm trying to see it as just a further questioning time with the judge that may or may not have an effect on the situation. So I keep my best case and worst case scenarios close together in my mind for balance. Only the baby knows how often I've held my breath.

It's erev Shabbos now. By the time you get this it will be erev Shabbos again. Have a good Shabbos each and every Shabbos. May Shabbos bring us many blessings for the week that follows. Love ya a whole bunch.

Miriam and Pitsy Witsy

Fear is a catalyst to forgetfulness — no wonder Miriam repeated herself often. She had been concerned and unsure of how to answer the psychologist, confused by what it had all meant. Desperately hoping that she had done well, she wanted information and reinforcement from the lawyer.

She had begun counting the days. This time, perhaps, they would let her keep her glasses and she'd be able to see the judge's face! Perhaps the judge would reveal something in her expression.

Miriam was afraid to be optimistic, but wouldn't allow herself to be pessimistic.

Sixteen more days. Sixteen long, hot, humid days.

Tears welled up as I thought about my daughter – young, pregnant, and in prison, choosing to be positive and able to find something to celebrate. How devastated she must have felt when neither the lawyer nor the chaplain came as she expected. Alone with her fears, having no one to address her concerns and questions; instead of depression (which is the choice I might have made), she focused on the card. Something she found beautiful that she could value and appreciate.

I found the situation unbearable. And I was not in prison — or perhaps I was.

44

"Just a Nisayon"

Dear Mom, Dad, and Josh:

Hello, precious family! I hope you're all doing well. There's not much new since Friday. But I'll tell you about my Shabbos. It was very nice. I lit at about 8:30,[6] which is early, but better early than late, G-d forbid! I had beef/rice for Friday night. It was yummy. Then I sang and learned from a book called Love Thy Neighbor with the baby. S/he is kicking a lot in the past two days. I guess the baby also likes Shabbos. It was so cool. Well, I fell asleep Friday night before I said maariv. So on Shabbos day I was going to definitely take a nap, but it was too noisy because of the kids playing in the nursery and I couldn't sleep.

I read Voices in the Silence, an inspirational book about a father imprisoned in Russia for two years. He refused to eat treif and his cell

---

6. The Sabbath is brought in by lighting candles eighteen minutes before sunset, but may be brought in by lighting earlier, especially in the summer months when the Sabbath begins late at night.

had no light or window. That is tzaros! What we have is just a nisayon. Baruch Hashem, we're able to be frum Jews. We're healthy. We are treated well. In the book, the father tells his daughter that everything that occurs in this world has a specific time decreed by G-d. Nothing is small when G-d decrees it to be big and vice versa. The quantity, quality, time, and place are all decreed by G-d. So when the time is right for the place to change, it will. We can daven to G-d that it will be soon. Because tefillos can change a decree.

Love,
Miriam and grandkid 2 be

Stories of others' imprisonments seemed to make their situation normal, easier.

At least they could get kosher food, pray, and continue to live a Jewish life. Miriam saw her observance as easy. I saw it as incredibly praiseworthy under such difficult circumstances. G-d was indeed holding her hand — or perhaps she kept her hand in His.

45
"Weighting" Game

Hi guys.

This is sort of a continuation of the last letter. I hope they come in order. Did Josh get the job he wanted?

I'm going to add salt to my food as you suggested to raise my blood pressure. Thank G-d, I'm not retaining fluids, so we'll try that. I'm also doing special exercises to move the baby closer to the front and off my back and arteries. So hopefully both should help. But worry not, I'm feeling good, thank G-d, and the baby is getting more active.

I'm happy you're hearing from Daniel often. Our present situation does cause many practical questions for our future.

After the hearing with the judge (which, with Hashem's doing, should go well), we'll have a better idea of the immediate future. Eventually, there will be a trial which at least Daniel (and most probably me, too) will have to attend. That might, G-d forbid, keep us here for some time. But one step at a time.

Oh, the nun is back from her vacation and it was nice to see her. We had an hour-long chat on Monday morning. She is a special lady.

I'm happy you feel that Daniel is growing from this too. Your opinion is important to me, and I'm always more pleased when you are too. I too sense his loneliness and wish so much that I could be with him through this. But like our rabbi wrote in a letter to Daniel, if we were together we wouldn't feel the pain. So, "no pain, no gain." That's from Pirkei Avos, did you know that?

Anyway, the gain we have already gotten (and with G-d's help what is to come) will overtake us and all pain will be forgotten. I tell the baby often how loved s/he is and by so many people. I hope and pray things work out — all things! Okay, I'll finish this and send it tonight.

Hi. It's 5:30 and supper's coming soon. After lunch I had powwow with those two visitors from the community. They brought three more novels, which I just received. Afterwards, I was called to "medical," where I had a quick exam. The doctor guesses that the baby is about 20 cm and maybe 1–2 kg. My blood pressure was 11/6. Back up in the "normal" range. I guess the salt and exercises have helped. She asked me if I'm eating cookies. No, I have no cookies.

I've gained a lot in the last five weeks, but in total it's not abnormal. The American baby book I have allows for a gain of 36 pounds in total. The European one allows only up to 32. I guess Europeans don't like to gain much. We listened to the heart again and it's good. She also measured my tummy and said I'm big, but good. I always have to ask.

She works silently, almost ignoring me. So I ask a bunch of questions and make her answer as much as possible. But I hope to get out of here soon and go to a regular doctor, who will see me as a person and not just a prisoner.

I had patchwork class today to make the decorative pillow. I cut out material for it already. When I was done at medical, there was only 20 minutes left to the class and I was tired, so I skipped it! I'll go next week — maybe only next week!

It's 12 days to our much-awaited date! I asked Daniel to fast that day and say extra tefillos and learn extra. I'll say as much Tehillim as I can. I don't know if I'll be allowed to take a Tehillim with me. I'll be away the whole day, even though the hearing is not long. Transport and waiting is the time consumer. So if you can get an idea of the time from the lawyer, maybe organize a special time for tefillah for us.

Anyway, we got lots of fruit with lunch today, including some watermelon! It's the second time. Yum!

Anyway, that's all over here. Please keep me updated on Bubby, and send her my love, and tell her we're davening for her and she must get better because I don't know her applesauce cake recipe! Okay, more reasons than that.

Well, lots of love. I haven't gotten any mail from Josh. Did he write?

Love ya,
Your daughter and kid

Twelve more days to go. Let's talk about Josh's job search. Let's talk about raising your blood pressure by adding salt to your diet as our doctor had advised. Let's talk about your return and being active. Let's talk about anything except the waiting...the long, long wait.

The doctor was asking questions about her diet, but she wasn't sure why. She had gained weight. Was that good or bad? Her question remained unanswered.

Patchwork class. Twelve more days. Tiredness. Twelve more days. No matter how hard she tried, the thought of twelve days came to the surface like a balloon underwater.

Meanwhile, my mom had congestive heart failure and was in intensive care.

46
"Deep Cholent"

Hello Mom, Dad, and Josh:

Hi guys. I'm sorry I didn't write yesterday, but the day actually flew by! I got a letter from Dad with graphics all over it. It was very colorful. I also got a beautiful card from Mom and the d'var Torah you sent, but I'm saving it for Shabbos.

Anyway, what did I do yesterday that the day went by so fast? Well, the morning is usually quick. 7:30: Take out garbage, get hot water, yogurt, shower. 8:15: Dress, eat, clean up room etc. 9:00: promenade (my shacharis time) till 10:00, then inside activity room. At 9:30, the mail came and there was a lot of it for me! So I went to my room to read it and finished davening.

I got two postcards from Rabbi K. In one he asks me for an idea for a speech he has to make on unity, so I thought of something. I meant to write him last night (but I fell asleep at 9:00). The idea is basically that first we note that am Yisrael is like one body. Each person being a piece: a limb, a finger, ear, toe, etc. Then we tell a

163

story of a young couple living within a beautiful community, till one group outside the community lies to and deceives this couple. They land in a big heap of trouble. A search-and-rescue immediately begins. They are found, trapped in a foreign country.

This couple survives this ordeal only as a result of the help from am Yisrael and because of ahavas Yisrael. The only way we as a whole can get out of exile, to bring Mashiach, and end galus, is with unity and ahavas Yisrael. If we see any sort of problem or tzaar in our fellows, our instinct should be to help them. We are part of one unit.

Okay, that's the basic. I'm going to write it as best I can and send it to him, and if he likes the idea, he can do it his way and make it really good. We will be giving chizzuk from our cells to a whole group of people through Rabbi K. I'm going to check over your letters again to see if there are any questions to answer.

My blood pressure is now 10/5. It went down a bit, but they say that it's because the baby is pressing on a main artery (normal) and causing a drop. Not to worry. I checked and my book says the same thing.

I'm so very happy you enjoyed the anniversary message. Wow, Mom had a good rest on Shabbos. Was that an anniversary gift from zopiclone? I'm glad the weather has cooled. Here too it's been cool, gray, and rainy, but oddly enough, the rain is great. My mood is super! Thank G-d. I think the trailer fund is a fantastic idea.

Betty is very nice, but still a stranger to me in some ways, so I'm hesitant. Mom, this isn't deep cholent, it's deep something else. If it were cholent, Daniel and I'd have gobbled it up and be out!

It's too bad that the clothes you sent are hiding somewhere. But I'd love the tops and the jumpers you bought. I hope they come soon so I can bring them home. Tikva and Betty came together on Monday, but Tikva didn't have a picture ID so they didn't let her up. She waited downstairs with her Tehillim while Betty and I had powwow.

Well, it's only 8:45 now. I rushed breakfast today to get this started since mail goes out at lunch. I'll leave some room in case there's any news by then.

Okay. Two letters and big d'var Torah from you. I'm happy to hear Mom's doing well. I hope Bubby too heals quickly and well, send her my love, she's in my prayers. I'm happy Meshulem shared his letter with you, especially since you didn't get mail that day. I'm so happy you won the lawsuit. Our mazal with courts should continue. Keep me updated with Josh's job situation. Check with Aaron. He probably knows people there too. Okay, I'm out of room.

The babies

The print of her letter got smaller and smaller as she filled every millimeter of paper. It was almost as if she didn't want to stop writing, stop holding hands.

"Deep cholent" was an expression we used at home for troubles. This indeed was way beyond "deep cholent."

"Trailer fund" — we loved camping, but our trailer had died of old age a few years before. We had decided to put away loose change toward a "trailer fund." Money had become very tight.

Zopiclone. Between the stress of my surgeries and my mother's illness and my daughter's imprisonment, sleep eluded me. I had begun taking a sleeping pill periodically for a respite from life.

The clothes had still not arrived. Now two boxes of maternity clothes were somewhere, but not where they needed to be.

The lawsuit. We had been taken to small claims court by the printers of her wedding invitations. They claimed we had given them an unlimited budget for invitations. We had paid them what they had said would be the maximum cost, plus tax. The judge ruled in our favor. Perhaps this was a good omen for judges.

As always, my Miriam remained a fountain of optimism – ever hopeful, praying for her freedom.

47

Coordinated Support

Dear Ta (aka Meshulem),

Thanks so much for your letter. I'd love to come to visit just so you won't miss me. (A few other reasons, too.) With G-d's help, we'll be home soon. It's perfectly fine with me to extend our contract till forever and a day!

Things here are the same. As we get closer to the 19th, my hope builds. I try to keep it in check so I won't be disappointed, G-d forbid. We anxiously await our date and daven for G-d to save us in any way He sees fit.

Your mother is always in my tefillos. I appreciate your offer to help, but it seems like all that can be done is being done. Please continue to be your beautiful self and be a source of friendship and encouragement to my parents.

I think that my father is affected by this the most. It is so hard for him because of his own limitations and the fears he has in the back of his mind, so please keep being the friend and support you've been. Thanks.

She enjoyed our friend Meshulem's letters. Their "contract" was an agreement made between them years ago for support. She was his honorary daughter. He was her "Ta" when she was away from home. His mother had taken ill. She was also in a nursing home, but the situation was grave. My mother continued to be in care, but the prognosis was better.

We were organizing prayers and *Tehillim* everywhere we could for July 19. They were to be said at the exact time she met with the judge. Meshulem played a large part in this.

48
Countdown

Dear Mom and Dad,

Hi guys. How's everyone feeling? Is it still good weather? How's your vision? How is Bubby doing?? Please send her my love. My prayers are filled with thoughts of all you guys. No more sicknesses! Okay? How is Josh?

Well, today I had a blood test for toxoplasmosis. We'll get the results later, but if all is okay (as we think) I won't hear anything. It's a routine test. My blood pressure on Wednesday was 11/6, so it's healthy again. I'm eating more salt and I do exercises to move the baby off my back.

I saw the lawyers this morning. They told me what's doing with the affidavits and that they're hopeful for the 19th. But let's try to keep calm. We don't know what will be! Whatever it is, we must remember that G-d is in charge and taking care of us. We must have complete faith! A girl was set free today. It was a surprise for her, so G-d's ways should continue.

I learned some Chumash yesterday with the Israeli girl here. It's her first time reading from a Chumash and we both explained parts to each other. I have my Chumash with me again, and maybe we can do more today.

I'm outside now. It's 2:15 and a beautiful day. Lots of sun and enough cloud and wind/breeze to keep cool. I just got called in to see the rabbi, so I'll just let you know that I love you guys a whole lot and we're both healthy and waiting to see you. I think as much as I need your love and support, Daniel needs it more. I thank G-d I have the foundation you built in me — strength, great faith, etc. So give him lots of love and Torah and encouragement, etc. Me, too, of course.

Okay, have a great Shabbos, one of comfort, relaxation, and a source of berachah for all Israel.

Love,
Miriam and Baby

Ten more days of waiting.

The affidavits were reference letters about us, Miriam and Daniel. They were from teachers, coworkers, friends, and professionals. There was also a sworn affidavit from their "friend" stating that Miriam and Daniel had no idea what they were carrying for him, no idea it was drugs. But would the judge believe him?

49
Holding Hands across the Miles

Dear Mama, Papa, and Josh:

Hi guys. It's Friday afternoon, I've had a busy day. Blood test, breakfast, shacharis, visit from the lawyers, lunch, cook for tomorrow, clean up, visit with the rabbi and promenade. It's now 4:30 and promenade is about to end. Then I have to take a nap, wash my floor for Shabbos, and do all my prayers (minchah, Shir HaShirim, Tehillim), then it's Shabbos! I just wanted to send you another letter today. How's Josh's job search? What's doing with Bubby? What nursing home? For how long?

Well, it's time to go in now. It's a beautiful day. Oh well, I've lots of work for Shabbos. Let's pray for a yeshuah for us and all of Israel, but we must keep in mind that G-d has a plan. We have been waiting for Mashiach for a long time, but we still believe he will come. So too, we must use that complete faith now to keep us strong, no matter what happens on the 19th!

Well, thank G-d, the baby is nice and active! Have a super Shabbos. Remember that we will soon be together. Everything has its time! A Shabbos of peace and blessings.

With love, hugs, and big fat kisses,
Miriam and Baby

The same. The same questions, the same words, letter after letter. Perhaps it numbed the anxiety for her. The letter could have had the alphabet written on it, I would still have cherished it. It was contact and as close to a hug as we could get. It was holding hands across the miles.

50

Betrayal and Its Domino Effect

Dear Mom, Dad, and Josh:

Hi guys. It's been a busy day. I'm waiting to go to powwow. This morning we awoke at 7:15 for showers and then had breakfast. I made oatmeal, but didn't have time to eat it, so I ate oatmeal with honey and raisins for lunch.

I got lots of mail today. A letter from you guys, three from Daniel, which explains why I got nothing on Friday or Shabbos. I got one from Reader's Digest saying I have a gift subscription from the Goldbergs — nice, right? If or when you speak to them, send my love. In a letter to Mrs. Goldberg, I tried to explain that until this is all over it's better not to write to them, because of their son's connection to our case. I am not angry with them at all. I don't hold them responsible for their son's actions. So I'd like to be clear that they're still very special to me and Daniel.

Well, now its 2:45 and I'm waiting to go over to the men's prison for another echograph! New pictures. I have to ask for them very nicely because they don't give them out to everyone. I'll try to get as many as I can. If I have only one, we'll send it to you so you can put it in the computer and make blowups. They're great!

That special report in the Jewish Press was very interesting! I hope it helps. Glad to hear you and Suzanne had fun shopping. Thanks for buying me stuff. I hope it gets here, and I hope the others are found!

Well, one week left till our big day! By the time you get this, we'll know what happened!

Pray good and remember that G-d is in charge here with a plan!

The Kids! (aka Miriam and the Grand)

Seven days left.

The parents of the friend who had set them up, the Goldbergs, had been in contact with Daniel and Miriam. So had his sister, who had been a close friend of my daughter. Letters and conversations had been difficult and awkward. Then the lawyers told us that we should sever all contact. The French authorities were searching for their son and had a warrant for his arrest. It made our children's innocence suspect if we were in contact with the family. How to separate the family from the "friend"? How to keep love of one while feeling anger, rage at the other?

The *Jewish Press* had featured an article warning people about taking packages even for friends or acquaintances. They told stories of others who had been duped. Some thought they were just helping friends by taking parcels, and others were being paid for carrying parcels of "gems" to avoid taxes and duty. Some were offered free trips just to pick up a business parcel because a nonexistent courier service had double-booked.

Whatever the ruse, the stories shared one common thread. All the people approached had only a few hours or less to decide if they would take the parcel or make the trip. Immediate decisions are necessary for the scam. Immediate decisions — before your brain kicks in and you realize something here is not quite right.

All the couriers, or "mules" as the police call them, had no idea they were carrying drugs. There were the five religious girls I had heard about who were delivering a birthday cake for a friend. The cake was full of drugs. There was the rebbe delivering a favorite brand of coffee for his student. The center of the jar was filled with drugs. And there were Daniel and Miriam, waiting in a French prison.

51
Hotel Paris

Dear Suzanne,

Thank you so much for your warm and friendly card. It was perfect! You sent me some smiles in the mail and they fit just right! Thanks also for the congratulations on the upcoming arrival. The baby has been growing a lot in the past little while, especially this past month. I've also been feeling it now for about two and a half weeks. What an amazing feeling.

My French has improved, but I'm far from fluent! Thank goodness for elementary school French. I know all the objects in a classroom! (Table, desk, chair, eraser, teacher.) It's the grammar that's tough. My sentences come out sounding like "I like to went outside."

So what are you all doing this summer? My husband and I are on an extended honeymoon in France! I'll bet you're jealous, huh! Well, you too can try this alternative lifestyle, but I wouldn't suggest it! The pillows aren't so great! Not to mention a few other things that are lacking.

Well, that's about it over here! I'll show you my pictures when I get home. We saw the Eiffel Tower, Arc de Triomphe, and took tons of silly pictures too. I can't wait to see them.

Well, keep on giving the wonderful support that you give to my Mom and Dad. I think this is harder for them than for Daniel and me. We're, thank G-d, healthy and doing well, and this "sabbatical" will eventually come to an end and we'll be home. If I can, I may have the baby at home and stick around for a few weeks. But those "plans" aren't for sure yet. We're just hoping!

Be well. I hope you all are. Good health, good friends/family are what are important, so thank you for being that good friend to me and Daniel and to my parents.

Take care of yourself and we'll see you soon!

Love,
Miriam

Friends, where would we be without them? Our friends continued to support Miriam and Daniel with letters and words of encouragement. Their support for them and us was overwhelming. And though they were few in number, they became an army of support.

And we waited...

Six more days.

52
Independence Day

Dear Mom and Dad,

Hi guys, it's Rosh Chodesh and I hope this new month brings good things to us and all of Israel! It's also France's Independence Day, so there was no mail. But Sister came especially to give me your message. She's a very sweet lady. So hugs and kisses back and I love you all lots, too. She gave me a hug from you. It's not exactly the same, but it was nice.

Well, I went yesterday for an echograph and the baby is growing nicely and everything is normal. I got no pictures, though. So I'm going to wait until next week and then request to see my doctor and ask her for one — if I'm here! I don't want to get my hopes up too high, so I'm not going to just think about time until Monday. Then, after Monday is finished, I'll turn my whole brain back on and allow myself to think of Tuesday, etc. For now I can only think up to Monday (or I'll go nuts!).

177

The baby is approximately 20 cm. That's like the width of this page, no? I don't have a ruler, so if you could show me what 20 cm looks like, that would be super. And boy, this kid is active. It's so amazing.

Well, I wrote to Bubby today. I got the address of the nursing home yesterday and the letter will go out tomorrow and get to Bubby's by Tuesday, I think. I think the rabbi is coming tomorrow, so he can give you fresh news. I had no visit today. I guess either because of Rosh Chodesh or because of France's holiday. Monday I am busy and I hope…oops, I forgot — end thinking on Monday!

Anyway, by the time you get this letter, it'll be almost Shabbos or the 9th of Av, so have an easy fast. Well, I'm going to leave some room for the morning in case I get something to tell you. See you soon, guys. Love you!

Well, not much new today. I did get mail from my favorite people, you guys and Daniel, so that was good. Nice card with the "love you more" in it. I really like it. I guess the rabbi will come tomorrow, so that will be nice. Thanks for the d'var Torah on Mattos-Masei. I'll read it on Shabbos. I also got a letter from Rabbi Cohen, nice and uplifting. Thanks for speaking to him.

Well, we're getting closer…every day is one day closer to the day we'll see you. Plus, we have the hearing on Monday so we'll get some sort of news! That's about it. We're feeling good and the baby is kicking lots. It's so nice to have a response from it. It's like confirming the fact that it's there and doing okay. Well, anyway, love you lots and hoping to see you soon!

Love,
Miriam and "little N"

P.S. Love to Josh and Bubby.

As July 19 approached, the separation between freedom and imprisonment became starker.

Miriam did not get echograph pictures this time. The little "inkblots" that had given her such joy had been withheld.

Kisses, hugs sent by messenger instead of firsthand. She wasn't able to put her head on my shoulder to cry and relieve some of her anxiety. I couldn't wipe away her tears.

One day at a time. Small steps. The fear — the hope — of Monday was untouchable, unthinkable. There was a barrier that stopped all thought past Monday. Thoughts of staying in prison, having her child in prison, were more than she could cope with or even think about right now.

Monday... Monday... ⁵³

Dear Mom, Dad, and Josh:

Hi guys. Well, I'm just getting around trying not to think about Monday. So much hope and yet I'm trying not to think about it. Whatever happens, Hashem gives us the tools to work with it, so we'll be fine! Anyway, not all that much is new. I have a runny nose, but I feel okay, thank G-d.

This little baby is kicking away. It's nice weather here. Mostly warm with lots of sun and enough cool days to keep me from getting too hot. On the 14th (France's Independence Day) a whole bunch of people got "Grace." It's sort of amnesty. If they're already judged and their crime isn't terrorism, murder, or drugs, they can be freed early. So the mood here is good. Well, I just got called to the rabbi, so I'll send love, hugs, lots of kisses for you.

Please let me know how Bubby is doing. I sent her a letter. Rabbi

A. brought the second package of clothes and I'll get it tomorrow.
Shabbat shalom, Shabbos peace and blessings.

Lots of love,
Miriam and Baby

The clothes had finally arrived! The second package was being delivered. The first was still somewhere on the ocean. At least now she had some clothes.

Something else to anticipate and look forward to, no matter what the judge would decide.

54
One More Day

With only one day left, we prayed that we would never see the return address of the prison on another letter – ever. She would see the judge tomorrow.

Strange, this new community we had become a part of, a prison community.

Not as different as we had thought. Girls saving their fruit for her, praying for her, caring for her.

The package of clothes was brought to her on Saturday. Because she couldn't sign for it on Shabbos, they took it away again. After waiting so long for the clothes, she had to wait one more day for that, too!

Waiting.

Tomorrow couldn't come fast enough.

55

Judge but No Judgment

Dearest Family:

Well, it's 12:20 a.m. so it's really Tuesday. I can't seem to sleep. I guess I'm all wound up from today. I'm sure the lawyers have filled you in and you probably know more than me at this point, but I'll tell you about my day.

They told me to be ready at 7:30. Since I was nervous, I woke up every hour from 3:00 on. I finally got up at 6:30 and started to get ready: dress, eat, daven, but at 7:15 they came so I didn't have time to daven, really. I took my Tehillim and some fruit and went to the search area.

Then at about 7:40, the van came. We made a few stops for pickups/ dropoffs and arrived at about 9:50. I waited until 11:00 and then spoke with the lawyers briefly. Then we all sat in the judge's office and she asked me questions. The interpreter of course had lots of work, but he's a nice guy. He even gave me some help! I guess in being afraid to say the wrong thing, I was saying very little. He told me to explain myself better and use emotion.

It was a great comfort to have the lawyers beside me (in their goofy robes). We didn't get to speak to each other during the hearing, but they'd nod or smile sometimes, which made me feel like I was doing okay. The judge was very casual and that, too, led to a more relaxed atmosphere.

So after all the questions, she said she'd think about it! Then the guard started to take me away. The judge said (through the translator), if she lets me go, I'll probably leave Wednesday or Thursday. The translator added what I think was his own piece — you're 90% free. I tried to see the lawyers' faces, but the guard was already walking with my hand attached to his cuffs, so I had to go!

So either they're telling me I'm free this week or my judge plays mind games! I'm in a very good but weird mood. I'm free but not free. It's strange. I'm in mental limbo.

Then I went back to the waiting cell till 9:00! I came back here and got mail, some food, etc. And the clothes! They're very nice. I'll wear them, with G-d's help, after Tishah B'Av since they're new.[7] So I'll have only a few days of waiting to wear them. The jumper with the flowers is so pretty and the tops are great.

So that was my big day. I hope the lawyers spoke to Daniel too because he was probably more wound up than me! I'm the laidback one, remember?

So by tomorrow, Wednesday, I should be told to start packing up or the lawyer better come see me! Maybe he'll come anyway tomorrow, for a follow up. See you soon, with G-d's help.

Miriam and Baby

This time she had her glasses and could see the judge.

The judge had refused to even consider bail for Daniel. She did not believe that any adult today could be so naive as to be given a package

---

7. New clothes are not worn from the Seventeenth of Tammuz until after the Ninth of Av because it is a time of mourning.

and not suspect drugs, even if it was arranged by a trusted friend. They would both be bound over for trial. But the judge did agree to consider bail for Miriam. Miriam had a sponsor and a job waiting. She would not be a burden on the French community. She would live with a French family, work as a teacher's assistant, visit her husband, check in regularly, and wait for her trial.

The judge would let Miriam know her decision in two or three days.

And so we waited some more.

There was no news on the first day or the second. The third day after seeing the judge was Tishah B'Av.

56
The Ninth of Av

The Ninth of Av. Disaster day on the Jewish calendar. The day of mourning for us throughout the centuries.

On the Ninth of Av, the golden calf was worshipped.

On the Ninth of Av, the spies returned from the Promised Land.

On the Ninth of Av, the First Temple was destroyed (586 BCE).

On the Ninth of Av, the Second Temple was destroyed and the exile began (70 CE).

On the Ninth of Av, the city of Beitar fell and thousands of Jews were brutally killed (135 CE).

On the Ninth of Av, Jerusalem was destroyed and replaced by the Roman city of Aelia Capitolina (136 CE).

On the Ninth of Av, Jews were expelled from Spain (1492).

On the Ninth of Av, Jews were rounded up and placed in the ghetto in Rome (1555).

On the Ninth of Av, the Warsaw Ghetto Uprising ended (1943).

And on the Ninth of Av Miriam waited, fearing the significance of this day and what it might mean for her.

On the Ninth of Av, the judge still had not responded...and it was the third day.

Miriam was fasting, despite being in her sixth month of pregnancy. She had read *Eichah* and sat on the ground and was explaining the significance of the day to some English-speaking girls. Depressed by the wait, by the heaviness of the day and what it would probably mean for her future. No wonder she didn't hear her name being called. They called again, ordering her to come in from the yard and report.

She got up and looked at the other girls. No one said anything. Slowly she walked to the door into the prison and the nursery.

She identified herself and looked at the guard's face for a hint of what awaited her. Nothing.

She was directed to the person she was to report to. The officer glanced up at her and spoke in French, without any emotion. He said, "You must go and pack up."

She froze.

"You go. You leave," the guard said in English.

"I can go?" she asked, afraid that she had misheard.

The guard smiled at her ambivalence. "Yes. Go."

She wanted to run outside and tell the girls, knowing how excited they would be for her. But they wouldn't let her go back. She had disappeared without word from the outside world when she was arrested. So too she would disappear from the prison, without a word, without a good-bye. But this time, everyone would know where she was.

The Ninth of Av. When Mashiach arrives, the Ninth of Av will be a day of rejoicing. Perhaps this was a small taste of what is to come.

Miriam was taken back to her cell and began packing. She gave her stove, the one she had awaited for so long, along with her pots and what remained of her food, to a fellow inmate who had nothing. She gave her toiletries to another whose kindness had been so welcome and some maternity clothes she no longer needed to a third. Her way of saying thank you for the help that had meant so very much to her from the beginning.

She was then taken to an office in the men's prison, a place she had never been. There, they unpacked everything, checked it over, and added the things that had been taken away from her when she was arrested: her wedding ring, the earrings Daniel had given her when they got engaged, and other confiscated items.

She was escorted through the yard to an exit that looked much like garage door. Freedom waited on the other side. She stood very still and stared as the door slowly inched its way open. On the other side stood a bearded man she had never seen before. Next to him was Betty. She stood very still. The world seemed to stop.

"*Allez*," said the guard. But still she stood her ground, fearful that if she moved, the door would close and she'd be locked in once again.

"*Allez*," he said again, this time motioning with his hands for her to go through the door.

"I can go?" she asked tentatively.

The guard smiled tolerantly. "Yes." He nodded and motioned with his hands once again. Slowly, as if in a dream, she walked toward the man and Betty, fearing that any minute the guard would order her return.

Betty hugged her and explained that this was the rabbi who had sponsored her. His family had vouched for her. She would be living with him, his wife, and their four young daughters.

She entered his car and wondered, yet again, at the help and trust of the French Jewish community. She was amazed that this man and his wife would take her, a complete stranger, into their home. Their generosity and trust was beyond her comprehension.

And it was the Ninth of Av.

Betty said good-bye and as the rabbi drove out of the prison complex, he handed Miriam his cell phone and said, "Perhaps you would like to call your parents?"

A few hours before, we had heard from the lawyer (who had been waiting for word at the prison) that she was to be released. The jungle drums, as I came to call the communication system in their old neighborhood, must have been going nonstop.

All morning, we received one call after another. Each call was interrupted by several call-waiting signals with good wishes, tears of joy, and words of excitement from people I knew and people I didn't know at all.

And it was the Ninth of Av.

The lawyer had hoped to see her when she was released. He wanted to introduce her to her sponsor and ease the transition. As the hours passed and she was still not released, he decided instead to go to the men's prison and let Daniel know that she was to be freed. The only way to tell him was directly. No phone calls, no messages were allowed — even from the lawyers. He had to be at Daniel's prison by four o'clock or they wouldn't let him in. He raced through the highway traffic, arriving at 4:05. They refused to admit him. And so Daniel would spend another day not knowing.

And it was the Ninth of Av.

My head was spinning from the calls. I had been on the phone for hours. I had no recollection of how many people I had spoken to, but a wonderful feeling of euphoria had taken over my very being. I apologized as I answered another call-waiting signal.

"Mommy?" The voice was tentative. "It's Miriam."

The sound of my daughter's voice, after so long. She was on the phone. That meant she was out, really out. I closed my eyes, unable to speak, and gave silent thanks.

And it was the Ninth of Av.

I kept her on the phone saying nothing, just wanting to hear her breathe, just wanting to stay connected. Finally she said she was using the rabbi's cell phone. She didn't want to add to his expenses. She would call from his house on a landline.

I smiled with pride. Some things never change. And some things do. Thank G-d.

And it was the Ninth of Av.

57
Healing Begins

Miriam's adjustment to freedom was slow and overwhelming. For four months, she had not been allowed to make decisions for herself. She had been ordered and regimented and instructed for so long that she had become accustomed to being institutionalized. There was even a strange comfort in it. The activity in her new home, with four wonderfully active young girls, was overwhelming. She often had to go to her room just to slow things down. The family was incredible, letting her adjust at her own pace and asking nothing of her in return.

She went out daily just to look at normal sights; to watch people walking, walking with purpose. She could go wherever she felt like going. Something she had forgotten and had to relearn. She looked into store windows and wondered, like a small child, at all that could be bought.

One day, about a week after she had been released, she called me. The excitement in her voice was bubbling over the phone line. "Mom," she said. "I did the most amazing thing today. It felt so great. I bought tomatoes and they let me pick them myself. It felt...it felt...incredible."

The healing had begun. It would take a long time for Miriam to return to the decisive, confident person she had been. It might even take years to repair the trauma. And what would become of Daniel? How long would he need? How many years of prison before his release? A year? Two? Longer?

But Miriam's healing had at least begun.

That was, unless the prosecutor decided to appeal the judge's decision. If she won the appeal, Miriam would be returned to prison immediately.

And to appeal was exactly what the prosecutor decided to do.

Again we waited, holding our breaths, celebrating each day of freedom as if it might be the last, and trying desperately to remember that G-d does not give us more than we can handle.

58
G-d's Gift

$\mathcal{I}$n August, France goes on vacation. Anything to do with the running of the government stops, including the penal system. And so the appeal that might send Miriam back to prison for months or years, to await her trial, was also put on hold.

As Miriam's due date neared, there were many decisions to be made. A boy would mean a bris. We never think of having a bris without the father present, yet how would that be possible in this situation? Day passes from prison were unheard of. Someone in the prison had recently lost his entire family in a car accident — his parents, wife, and children all perished in the terrible crash. And yet he was not allowed to attend the funeral and say good-bye. How would they ever allow Daniel to come out to greet his son?

Still, the lawyer said he would try, but first we needed to know the gender of the child, as there was no reason to begin a long, tedious, difficult process if it wasn't needed. Having a girl would make things much simpler.

The lawyer arranged for Miriam to take a test that would tell them whether they were having a boy or girl. Determining the gender before birth wasn't commonly done then, and I remember Miriam's excitement as we entered the doctor's office.

I had flown to France again to be with her while we awaited the baby's birth. As I sat in the waiting room, I prayed silently that it would be a girl. I could not begin to imagine how we would make a bris in this foreign place, where I couldn't even communicate with most people. Where would it take place? Who would be there? How would I get my wheelchair-bound husband here, to France? To miss such an event would be so painful for him. To have a *simchah*, such a wonderful celebration, without those closest to you there, diminishes the joy. This was to be his first grandchild.

And what of Daniel? He would be sitting behind prison walls while his son went through his bris without his father. It was too painful to even think about.

It would be a girl. I was sure of it.

As I waited for Miriam and the results, my mind began to wander. Leaving the French magazines for others who could read them, I thought about my granddaughter and prayed she would be born in freedom and Miriam would not be taken back into custody to deliver her child chained to a bed with no husband present.

I thought of how spoiled we are, always assuming the father will be at the bris. I was amazed at how much we take for granted in our daily lives and how quickly things can change. Of course it would be a girl. Oh, please G-d, a girl. How would we possibly do a *pidyon haben* without the father? Yes. A girl. I was sure of it.

Miriam exited the doctor's office with a glow. She seemed to float as she came close and put her arms around me. "It's a boy!" she whispered. "I am so excited! It's a boy."

My heart sank, but I forced myself to smile. Miriam was so happy, so thrilled. I would not take away this moment of joy.

"Let's go celebrate," I said, forcing myself to mirror her happiness. "Lunch and clothes shopping for us!" I reminded myself for more times than I can remember that G-d does not give us what we cannot handle. We would handle this, somehow. G-d would show us how and we would handle this, too.

A few days later I left France, returning home to care for my husband, check in on my mother, connect with my son, and make arrangements to return for the birth of my first grandchild.

59
The Pledge

I had made a *neder*, a pledge, that if Miriam was freed on bail I would donate a month's salary to our shul. We davened in a small synagogue with few members, and membership fees rarely covered the operating expenses. Donations were always welcome.

I had tried several times to drop in to see the rabbi and make the donation, which was a bizarre amount. I had taken my yearly salary and divided it by twelve months, arriving at a substantial number of dollars and 71 cents. I decided not to round off the amount. I had pledged a month's salary and that was what I was determined to donate. I dropped into the shul several times, but each time the rabbi was away.

Weeks passed and still I had not made the donation. I was determined to redeem it before my return to France. Finally, we connected. It had been so many weeks ago that I made this pledge. The rabbi looked at the check and shook his head from side to side and made some incomprehensible murmurings.

Finally he told me to sit down. He told me how just that week he had been pressured to pay some outstanding synagogue bills. He had tried several avenues but could not seem to get the money together. He had no further ideas on how to raise the money that needed to be paid by nightfall. That morning, he had decided to leave the problem in Hashem's hands.

My donation was the exact amount he needed — to the penny! He was amazed. G-d had arranged the timing perfectly yet again. I saw it as another miracle that surrounded us in this saga. All we had to do was be willing to see it.

And there were so many more miraculous events, which I didn't see coming, that were on their way.

60

Two Powerful Losses

*A*s Miriam's due date approached, I booked my ticket to return to France to be with my daughter. My husband's condition remained stable and my mother's health was improving. My mother had been so worried about my daughter and so ill over the last while that I opted for a two-week stay in New York, to spend time with Mom, before flying on to France.

My mother's passing coincided with the time of my visit. Instead of a visit, I buried my mother and sat shivah in her home. I missed her terribly and was pained that she missed the birth of her first great-grandchild by only weeks. But the timing of her passing filled my mind with questions. I could not help but wonder what I would have done had she passed away while I was on another continent and my daughter was giving birth. Who would I be with? Could I go home to bury my mother and leave my daughter alone to give birth in France? How would she have managed? G-d continued to hold our hands through the good events and bad, arranging everything in our favor.

After shivah, I flew to France to support my daughter, who would soon know whether she or the prosecutor had won the appeal. We still pretended everything was normal. Each day we explored the city and dined as if this was our last meal together. It very easily could be.

The lawyer called me on a rainy afternoon to tell me she had lost the appeal. We'd be notified when the prison guards would come to get Miriam. She asked me to tell my daughter. Having to tell her she was to be returned to prison broke my heart.

How many times can a mother's heart be broken? I begged Hashem to spare me the painful sight of watching my pregnant daughter being led away in handcuffs. Yet leaving her to deal with this alone, without support, without me holding her hand, was not an option.

Each day we waited for the notice from the prison. We went out for dinner knowing it would probably be our last meal together. We waited and waited, but the first week passed and still we heard nothing.

Miriam was required to check in at the police station once a week to prove she was still in France. The police expressed surprise when she came. They showed her the paper that stated she would be returning to prison, although there was no date. They said she would probably hear something that week, but gave her an appointment to check in with them the next week, just in case.

This scenario repeated itself the following week, and the week after. We continued to go out each night, fearing it would be the last time we were together. She went to the police station to check in and they expressed surprise at seeing her. "You're still out?!" they exclaimed. They gave her an appointment for the following week but assured Miriam she'd be in prison by then. And this scenario continued and Miriam remained free, as long as she didn't leave France.

Much later we discovered that the appeal decision had been misfiled. It had gotten stuck on a Post-it note and was lost in her prison folder. This miracle kept Miriam out of prison until the trial. Hashem had answered my prayers again.

61

Wait! Don't Wait!

A s Miriam's due date neared, the lawyer told us the protocol for going into labor in France. He told us not to tell the cab driver where we were going until we were seated in the cab.

"If they think you're in labor when you call for a cab, they will simply not pick you up," he said. Hailing a cab on the street might have the same results. They might just drive on. If desperate, he told us to call the fire department.

I wasn't sure how to call a cab in French, much less the fire department. How was I to deal with this? But it became almost a nonissue: Miriam's due date had come and gone. Her doctor saw her frequently. The baby was large. The doctor wanted to induce, fearing the pressure to the baby's head might cause problems in labor. In the United States at that time, doctors usually waited two weeks after the due date to induce labor. In France they generally induced closer to the due date. The decision — induce or wait — was Miriam's.

Everyone bombarded Miriam with their opinion. *Wait! Don't wait!* Miriam and Daniel discussed it on her frequent visits to the prison, neither of them knowing what to do. I refused to voice my opinion

199

unless asked. Being free is not just about physical freedom from prison. It is the freedom to make decisions for yourself, without pressure from everyone around you. And, as with any issue with which they had to deal, there were many opinions and a lot of pressure.

Three days later, Miriam turned to me and asked what she should do. Invited in, I told her to follow her heart and her mind. I asked her if she trusted her doctor and believed what her doctor said. I mentioned that the thinking from home didn't include anyone who had seen her as a patient. But in the end, it was their baby and they would deal with whatever happened, so they needed to decide what was right for them.

Miriam decided to follow her doctor's advice and go for the induction. She was given an appointment at the birthing clinic for two days later. She would work with her doctor's midwife until the baby was ready and then the doctor would appear.

Neither of us slept much the night before the appointment. My concerns — along with the serious ones for my daughter and her baby's health and welfare — included being able to get a taxi in the morning to take us to a birthing clinic once we had given him the address. But there were no problems, except it seemed to me the taxi driver drove quite quickly through the streets and discharged us with great haste and relief.

In that lovely French birthing clinic, on a beautiful Tuesday morning, we were blessed with our first grandchild, weighing in at nine and a half healthy pounds. The child looked exactly like Daniel.

Once Miriam was taken to her room, her nurse noticed how responsive the baby was to his mother's voice and how quickly he was comforted by her words. She said that she only sees that when mothers take the time to talk and sing and connect with their child constantly before birth. She wondered how Miriam had found the time. Smiling, we left the question unanswered.

62
Just in Time

After taking several pictures of the baby, I ran to find a pay phone to call Monsieur Edouard, the volunteer from CADI, who had arranged to visit Daniel that day. I wanted Daniel to know that everything had gone well and mother and son were fine. I wanted him to know the baby looked exactly like him. I felt the more information he had, the less pain he would experience from not having been there.

Since I didn't speak French, no one I asked was able, or perhaps willing, to direct me to a public phone. I finally found one, but it was out of order. I ran up and down the streets outside the birthing clinic to try to find a phone booth. I kept looking at my watch. I didn't know when Monsieur Edouard had made his appointment to see Daniel. Once he was in the prison, I would not be able to reach him, and Daniel would not know that everything had gone well.

I passed several broken phones until, with sweat pouring down my face, I found one that worked. I reached Monsieur Edouard just moments before he entered the prison complex. If it had been just minutes later, I would not have been able to give Daniel the news that he had a healthy son and all was well. I cannot imagine the torture and doubt he would have gone through that night until I could visit the next day to tell him all was well.

G-d had been good to us once again.

63
Breaking All the Rules

I had arranged to visit Daniel the next morning. I knew he would want to know every detail of what had occurred. Once Miriam and my new grandson were settled in the birthing clinic, I headed back to our apartment, but first stopped at a store that developed pictures overnight. I was determined to show Daniel pictures of his new son. The price for overnight film development was exorbitant, but there cannot be a price too high for a father to see his newborn son.

I didn't sleep much, whether from excitement or fatigue or worry about what I intended to do the next day. I watched the hands on the clock as the hours passed. I didn't need the alarm to wake me. I left very early, taking the Metro to first pick up the pictures and then begin my trek of over two hours on the Metro, the long-distance train, and finally the bus to the prison that housed Daniel. During the ride, I kept looking at the pictures, deciding which two I would smuggle in for him to see.

I arrived at the prison with not much time to spare before my appointment. I deposited everything into the locker except the two pictures I had chosen. I took them into the bathroom and carefully hid them in my clothing. It was forbidden to bring anything into the visiting room. I did not know the penalty I would receive if I was caught bringing in these pictures. I didn't want to know. I just knew I had to do it. It would be beyond cruel if Daniel could not see his child.

I went in with my group of visitors. I passed the metal detector without problem and, thank G-d, there were no personal searches that day. Once in the tiny locked room, I took out the pictures and put them in my lap under the table and waited for Daniel to arrive.

When he was brought in, I could see the joy and anxiety written on his face. I took out the pictures. Through tears and laughter, he lifted the pictures of his newborn son and kissed them. I retold him in detail the events of yesterday, so that he could feel as much as possible as if he were there.

The guards began to come by to check on the prisoners and their visitors, as they did every few minutes. I was concerned about the pictures and asked Daniel to put them out of sight, but he refused. Instead, he called the guard in and asked him in his broken French, which even I was able to understand, about keeping the pictures. He told him it was his new baby, his son, just born.

I was petrified, wondering at the consequences of my act of defiance to the prison rules. Much to my shock, the guard allowed him to keep one picture but took the other. He left us, amid our outpouring of thanks, to continue our visit. G-d had held our hands once again.

The visit over, I went outside to wait for the bus that would take me to the long-distance train. The skies were black and torrential rains had started sometime after I had entered the prison. I had a coat, but no umbrella, hat, or hood. I waited and waited at the bus stop, but no bus arrived. Finally, another visiting family saw me and realized my dilemma. They came over and explained in broken English and with sign language that the bus, for some reason, was not running now.

I walked back to the guard station to call a taxi, only to discover that it had already closed. The phone was locked inside with the prisoners.

I stood wondering what to do. No way to call a cab. No buses running. It was dark and the rain seemed to have no mercy.

I began to walk towards the highway, hoping I could remember the route the bus took as it headed back to the station. I hoped it would remain light enough for me to see where I was going. Maybe a cab would pass as I walked along what I hoped was the correct way.

As I headed for the highway, a young man came running up to me. I recognized him as someone who had been in my visitor group several times, though we had never spoken. He asked me in broken English if I was going to the train station and offered me a ride in his car. I readily accepted, all the while thinking of how often I had warned my children about accepting a ride from strangers, strangers who were visiting criminals no less. Just like me.

He had a two-door car and a friend was in the passenger seat. I climbed into the rear of the car feeling momentarily grateful, but a bit ill at ease. I suddenly remembered what I had recently read in the book *The Gift of Fear* — how women instinctively know when they should be fearful and need to listen to that inner voice. Instead society socializes them to disregard that instinct, just as I had. Doing so takes away from them their natural self-protection.

Climbing into the driver's side of the car, the young man turned on the cassette player. Arab music began to blare. The two men sang along, and I began to become more concerned about what I had just agreed to. I had no way of getting out of this two-door car should I need to make a quick exit. What could I do to help myself if I was subject to foul play? I had no escape route.

My mind began staging an internal argument. On one hand, it told me, I could be robbed and murdered or worse, left at the side of the road and no one would know. I might never see my beautiful new grandson again. In response, the other side of my brain tried to insist these were just good Samaritans helping out.

As I debated, they began driving. Very quickly, it became clear to me that they were not headed in the direction of the train station. I asked where they were headed as we passed an empty field and my heart pounded in my chest. They insisted they were going to the train, but I was sure, because I have a good sense of direction, that they were headed in the opposite direction.

I sat quietly offering silent prayers and deals, asking G-d to ensure my safety, when the car stopped at a location I had never seen before. There, in front of me, was a major train station I didn't know existed. They told me this train would take me back to Paris much more quickly than the other station I had used — but you could only reach it from the prison by car.

I exited the car with words of thanks to my drivers. I thanked G-d for my safety and for having sent me the good Samaritans. My heart, though, was still in crisis mode and refused to slow its pounding.

Soaked from rain and shaking from the frightening situation I had just put myself through for no reason, I got directions to the Metro stop that would take me to the birthing clinic. Wanting to just go back to my bed and hide under the covers until normalcy returned to my life, I headed into Paris to visit my daughter and new grandson.

64
The Unfunny Joke

I must have been quite a sight when I entered my daughter's room that night. She had visitors with her, old friends of ours who happened to be in Paris on business and had come with gifts for the baby. I walked in and the conversation came to an immediate halt.

I don't think it was just my physical appearance that stopped the conversation. Yes, I was soaked through from the rain and exhausted from the experiences of the last few days. But when one of the guests immediately brought me a chair, I wondered if I looked as if I would pass out. I suspected the fear of being arrested in the prison because of the baby pictures as well as the trauma resulting from the unscheduled car ride still showed on my face. I realized that I was shaking still.

I told them the story.

"Mom!" My daughter was shocked. "How could you do that? How could you take a ride when you had no idea who they were? After all you taught us..."

"How could I not?" was my response and I began to laugh. "Would it have been safer for me to walk along the road in the dark trying to find my way to the train station? I'd probably still be walking!"

Warmth returned to my body as I held the new baby. The conversation turned light and happy as we all enjoyed watching the newborn. I was grateful for the safety of being in a place with people I knew, trusted, and loved, and very thankful to hold my delicious new grandson, this new life, this miracle.

As we were all leaving so that the new mom could rest, my friend handed me a package. "This is for Daniel," he said.

"I no longer take packages for anyone," I said. "Not even for a good friend!" We all laughed at the joke that really wasn't funny at all.

65
Planning the Festivities

S hortly after we discovered that Miriam was having a boy, I received a call from Aaron.

"What does your husband need to get to Paris for a bris?" he asked with his hallmark energy that always makes the impossible seen doable and easy.

"Forget it!" I answered. "It can't be done. It's too difficult and complicated."

But my answer only heightened Aaron's determination to make sure Reuben would be there. I started to enumerate what would be involved in getting a paraplegic on an international flight. He would need an attendant. First-class tickets near a bathroom were not a luxury but a necessity. Handicap transportation from the plane and an accessible hotel were at the top of the list. Then the bris would have to be held in an accessible location. The list went on and on.

Reuben and I had long ago given up any thought of his ever seeing his grandchild until Miriam was able to return home, whenever that would be. But Aaron insisted it could and would be done. He was so persuasive that Reuben became involved in the planning.

A few days later, early in the morning, two open first-class tickets to Paris arrived by courier. One for Reuben and one for the orderly we had used to assist us in traveling to Miriam's wedding. The tickets had been sent by an anonymous donor. To this day, the identity of that amazingly sensitive person remains unknown to us.

Suddenly, what was a fantasy quickly became a reality. Reuben began to work on accessible transport in Paris, while I looked for wheelchair-friendly hotels. We even discovered that Reuben would be able to visit Daniel, as the prison he was in was wheelchair accessible. We purchased a ticket to Paris for Josh. Miriam would be without her husband, but she would have the full support of her family.

Tikva and her husband were invaluable in making the bris. They insisted that it be in their home. They lived on the eighth floor, but the entrance to the building was level and the building had an elevator. We found an accessible hotel one block from their apartment building. Things were falling into place easily...and miraculously.

Tikva and her husband had a friend who had taken an interest in my children's situation. Claude had had his own experience with the French prison system years before and had a keen understanding of how being innocent doesn't exempt you from the pain of being incarcerated.

It seems that someone had used Claude's office, without his knowledge, to do some illegal business. Claude was picked up and arrested for the crime. It was a few days before Rosh HaShanah when he was placed in prison. The authorities didn't bother to let his family know. His wife was nine months pregnant at the time. Claude fell into a deep depression in the prison. He worried about his wife. What would she think of his disappearance? What of his new unborn child? And here it was, Rosh HaShanah. He longed to hear the sound of the shofar.

Claude was reciting the New Year's prayers when he thought he heard the shofar blasts and was sure he was losing his mind. But his cellmates called him to the window and there, outside the prison and not far from their cell window, was a rabbi blowing the shofar for all to hear. What's more, it was a rabbi who knew Claude.

Claude screamed to get his attention. Once he did, he asked him to let his family know where he was and enlist their help. And that is how Claude's wife discovered that her husband had been arrested.

Claude and his wife insisted on making the *vach nacht* in their home the night before the bris. The night before a boy's circumcision is considered a spiritually dangerous time, and one holds what is often called a *vach nacht* to provide the baby with additional protection. Children come to say prayers with the baby. The father, if present, gathers a minyan to learn Torah and a festive meal is served.

Claude and his wife did it all for our new grandson. We enjoyed many Sephardic dishes and wonderful company, and felt as if the protection was as much for our family as for the baby. It was a wonderful evening, in an apartment building that miraculously featured an elevator (rare in that neighborhood) so that Reuben could be present. Reuben glowed as he learned with the other men and felt he could play a part in the protection of his grandson. Daniel's presence was the only thing missing.

As I look back at those few days, I am as amazed now as I was then at the kindness of people I had only known for a short time or didn't know at all. The goodness of ordinary families who barely knew us but wanted to help in whatever way they could. And I have boundless gratitude to Hashem, who kept holding my hand as I continued to put one step in front of the other. I thought back to the anguish I had felt when I first heard that Miriam was having a boy. I was embarrassed by my momentary lack of faith. I should have known that G-d would see us through this, as He had at every turn.

66
An Uplifting Miracle

A few of Daniel and Miriam's friends had come to Paris to be with them for the bris and lend support. That morning, Tikva had taken her children to school early, and I was preparing the wonderful array of food she had ordered. I had no idea that we were facing another dilemma until Rachel, Aaron's wife, came into the apartment pale and out of breath.

"What's the matter?" I asked.

"I don't know how to tell you this." A pause. "But...the elevator is broken. It just won't work!"

What was I going to do now? How could we get Reuben up eight flights of stairs? Everything had been so perfect — and now this.

While I was trying to figure out how I could possibly make this work, Reuben and Josh moseyed into the apartment. I was dumbfounded.

"How did you get up here?" I asked.

Josh looked at me as if I had just landed on this planet and said in his most patient and patronizing tone, "There is a small box called an elevator. You open the door and go inside. Then you press a button corresponding to the floor you want, and *poof!* you're here."

"But the elevator's broken!" I insisted.

"Mom. We're here, aren't we? What are you talking about?"

The elevator worked only twice that day. Once to get my husband and son up to Tikva's apartment, and once to take them down. It did not work the rest of the day, and stayed broken for another month. G-d was indeed holding our hands.

Later, Tikva told us that when she took her children to school early that morning and discovered the elevator wasn't working, she took G-d to task. All the while she was driving, she argued with Hashem. "You cannot do this! Her father has come all this way! He cannot miss the bris! It just cannot be! You must do something!"

And He did.

67
Humble Mohel, Reluctant Sandak

M iriam and Daniel needed to decide who would be the *mohel*, who would circumcise their son. They had prominent *mohelim* who offered to come short and long distances to do the mitzvah. But they wanted someone who would approach this occasion with simplicity. They wanted this bris to be like thousands of others, without celebrity status and with the focus on the baby, the mitzvah, and not the circumstance.

And so they chose a very humble gentleman, a pediatrician who had agreed to look after their son and who also happened to be a *mohel*. He was a man with beautiful *middos*. He was very kind, and an aura of softness surrounded him. Quiet, never on show, his ego was never involved in the advice he gave or the care he encompassed them with. It was a "normal" bris, with no fanfare.

There was a minyan of men in attendance, and a small group of local people with whom they had become close. Josh, Reuben, and I and a handful of friends from home who surprised Daniel and Miriam completed the small gathering. The event was low key and focused on the baby and the mitzvah, just as they wanted it to be. I was glad, once again, that I had left the decision to them. It was my gift, returning a bit of control to their lives when so much had been taken away.

There was no question in anyone's mind that the *sandak*, the person who has the honor to hold the baby during the ceremony, would be Aaron. He had done so much for them. He had found them when they disappeared and arranged for lawyers and, through them, their kosher food. He was the eye in the storm, always present and leading us in the appropriate direction.

He adamantly refused the honor. Humility not being the only reason. It seemed that Aaron could not deal with the sight of blood. He was afraid he would faint while holding the baby. But we were as strong in our insistence as he was in his refusal. Finally, he agreed. We advised him to look upward and not at the baby during the bris.

It was not until the baby was given his name that we realized that Aaron had indeed passed out, and was sitting, unconscious, with the baby on his lap.

Everyone reacted at the same time. Grabbing the baby so he wouldn't fall, holding Aaron up so that he too wouldn't be hurt, while others yelled to lay him on the floor. Momentary chaos won out.

Aaron's wife, Rachel, immediately ran to the kitchen to get water to revive him. On her way she passed a table of perfumes (this was Paris, after all) and grabbed the first bottle and the wet cloth that was beside it, thinking it was wet from water. She proceeded to spray Aaron's face with eau de toilette and wipe his forehead with a cloth reeking of pine sol until he was revived, which did not take long with this cacophony of odors.

Baby and *sandak* were fine. To Aaron's chagrin, we have it all on video.

68
Pidyon in Prison

The pediatrician advised that the baby not go to the prison to see his father until after he had his shots. At Daniel's prison, all visitors waited in a small, confined space until allowed in for the visit. There were people from all over the world in that area, and he was concerned that the baby, before being immunized, might be exposed to several diseases. And so Miriam, once she felt stronger, went to visit Daniel alone when she could.

The next question we encountered was how to perform a *pidyon haben*. How were we going to have a *pidyon* for my grandson? Not only was the child's father incarcerated, but he also had nothing of value on him with which to do the redemption. We could not bring him anything when we visited and anything of value, like five silver coins, if sent to him, could easily disappear. And where would we get a *kohen* to complete the ceremony? We asked the local rabbi, who had helped us all along, how to proceed.

And just as so many times before, everything miraculously fell into place. Daniel's lawyer was a religious Jew who, we discovered, happed to be a *kohen*. In fact, he often performed the *pidyon* ceremony in his community. He consulted with the rabbi on how to conduct the ceremony in prison, when the father has no possessions, there is no minyan, and the baby is not present. After much discussion and consultation with other Jewish authorities, they came up with a plan.

The lawyer made an appointment to see Daniel on the thirtieth day after the baby's birth — the day on which the *pidyon* was due to be performed. Not being able to bring with him to the visiting cell anything but tools of his trade, he brought with him a gold pen. The lawyer told Daniel that the pen was a birthday gift from him to Daniel, and Daniel had to accept it with sincerity and take possession of it. Once Daniel accepted the pen as his own, he could use it to redeem his child. And so the ceremony took place between them, and our grandson was redeemed.

The rabbi called me a few days before the ceremony was to take place. "I thought you'd like to know," he said "that when the child is not present at the *pidyon*, there is no *seudas mitzvah*."

I felt instant relief. I had wondered how I would possibly put together another festive occasion. A party was the last thing I had the mental or physical energy to do. And yet to have no celebration seemed anti-climactic.

Miriam and I discussed it, and she liked my idea. We would go out to dinner and take their other lawyer, the female lawyer, as our guest. And so we celebrated another rite of passage; just ourselves, the lawyer, and, of course, the guest of honor, who slept peacefully in his car seat the whole time.

69
Hope of Freedom

T hough my grandson was only a few weeks old, the lawyer
insisted we get him a passport. Should they deport Miriam
instead of sentencing her, he wanted to make sure she and the
baby headed for the airport immediately. Once again, he feared the
prosecutor, who had succeeded in overturning the judge's decision. He
told us there had been cases where the prosecutor had succeeded in
pulling people off the plane before it was airborne so that they would
serve time for a judgment that had originally meant freedom and she
had succeeded in reversing.

We went to the American Embassy to apply for a passport. By the
time we arrived, though it was quite early, there was a line of people
waiting to get into the embassy. The queue was already around the
block.

We almost mistakenly joined that line, but as we walked down the
street looking for the line's end, we saw the sign at a second entrance
that stated this other entrance was for US citizens only. Two guards
stood by that door, and there was no line at all. I began to realize how
lucky we were to have been born American. Perhaps for the first time I

marveled at how many people were trying to get into my country and how precious my citizenship was.

After stating our business, we once again saw the wonderful service officer who had been very helpful through this whole ordeal. He gave us the appropriate papers and gave us the letter we needed to apply for a rush passport. We filled out the papers and attached the proper documents, and were then directed to the embassy's passport photo machine. We stopped along the way to feed the baby and get ourselves a drink, and by the time we got there we discovered that the photo machine was broken.

The lawyer wanted the passport in his hand immediately, so we asked what we could do to get the photo taken that day. We were directed to a private photographer not terribly far from the embassy.

Off we went. We found the shop. The photographer sat my daughter in a chair and promptly threw a sheet over her face and body. He then placed the baby on her lap so that only her hands, holding the baby, were showing.

The photographer asked us if we needed a picture for a French passport, as well. He assumed we would be applying for one, since the child was born in France and could apply for French citizenship should we want it. We politely declined.

US passport photo in hand, we walked back to the embassy and completed the process. We walked out of there with a passport for a five-week-old.

When we emerged, the line around the embassy by Frenchmen and immigrants to France was twice the size that it had been that morning. I joked with my daughter that we could probably sell the passport and not only recoup the money their "honeymoon" to France had cost, but make a profit as well.

We both laughed, but we knew the document was worth much more than any dollar value. It was our symbol, our hope of freedom to come.

70

Being Vulnerable Again

*L*eaving the baby in my care, Miriam visited Daniel whenever she could. One ill-fated day she emerged from the long-distance train, which arrived a few minutes late, to see the local bus pulling away. The next bus that went to the prison was scheduled to arrive too late for her to make her appointed visiting time.

She tried hailing a taxi, but none were available. Having no alternative, she ran the bus route all the way. When she arrived, sweaty and out of breath, her group was just being assembled. She could have easily joined them, but the guard refused to allow her to enter.

She argued with him in her broken French. She pleaded and explained that she had missed the bus and couldn't get a taxi, but the more she begged and explained, the more intransigent he became. Having absolute power over others can bring out kindness or it can motivate others to exercise complete control and punishment. This guard, unfortunately, chose the latter.

She returned home exhausted and depressed. A delay of less than five minutes had taken away a visit with Daniel, and she was unable to see him that week. The incident made us realize, again, how vulnerable we were and how cruel people can be if they choose to be.

I left my daughter once again and headed home. Tikva and her family had invited Miriam to live with them when I had left. (While I was there, we stayed together in an unused apartment offered to us by a member of the French Jewish community.) There was no end to the love and caring shown to us by this incredible community. It made my leaving Miriam and my new grandchild easier, though not easy. I knew they would be well cared for by these wonderful people while she awaited the trial. And, even more important, she would not be alone.

Despondent, I wondered how long it would be before they set a trial date. I resumed my routine, returned to work, and pretended life was normal.

Meanwhile, Miriam developed her own routine. Once the baby had his shots, she began to take him to see his father. Tikva drove her to the prison when she could. Always aware of the financial burden we had shouldered in caring for her and Daniel, Miriam rarely spent the money we sent her for taxis. Instead, she continued to commute the exhausting two-plus hours each way on public transportation with the baby.

At home, we waited for the trial date as anxiously as we had waited for the bail hearing. Each day we hoped for news and heard nothing, but at least she remained free as long as she stayed in France. The return-to-prison card was still elusive.

The lawyers tried to move up the trial date. Once the trial was over, we would at least know what we were dealing with.

Miriam's routine continued, as did mine. I flew to France for another visit and was invited by Tikva to stay with them all just before they left on a family vacation. They made me as welcome as they had my daughter. Their home stretched to accommodate us, and their daughters insisted they absolutely loved to share a bedroom.

After they left for their vacation, they insisted we stay on. I savored my time with my grandson and daughter, and we both pretended we were on vacation, doing our best to avoid thinking about what was coming. Time passed too quickly, and before I realized it I had to return home. And still there was no trial date.

I had never appreciated being able to use a phone as much as I did once Miriam was out. We talked every day, a luxury we hadn't had when she was in prison. It saddened me to think that she and Daniel could only communicate through letters and their half-hour visits three times a week. This was their second year of marriage; most of their married life had now been spent behind bars. I wondered when normalcy would return to their lives, and if and how they would adjust.

Finally, we heard from the lawyer. A trial date had been set. I mentally prepared to pack my bags again. Although petrified of what I might witness, I was more frightened of having Miriam and Daniel go through this alone.

But the lawyer was adamant. I was not to come. He wanted Miriam to be alone in court. He wanted the judges to see a very young woman — a girl really — who had no support. He hoped this would help, should they want to sentence her to a long prison term. He wanted it to appear as if there was no one to care for her child, who was only a few months old and totally dependent on her. This baby would have no choice but to be with his mother in prison, and should they sentence her, the judges would be responsible for that. He told her to make sure the baby cried a lot and to nurse him frequently.

On the day of the trial, people gathered to say *Tehillim* for them — both people who knew them well and those who had just heard about their story. To this day I have no idea who organized this or if it was spontaneous. I just knew it was happening and thanked G-d with every fiber within me. I begged Him to hear the pleas that were being sent in His direction on behalf of my children and answer them favorably.

I spent that day praying and sitting by my phone, pleading that it would ring with good news. We jumped every time the phone rang and hung up quickly when it was not the call we waited for. For the second time, I sat by the phone waiting to receive the call that would tell us of my children's future.

71
The Trial

Not having been present, I had no idea how the trial proceeded. When I discussed it with Miriam, she recalled little, if anything, of the procedure. She remembers feeling great fear. She remembers constantly asking Hashem for His help for herself, her son, and her husband. She said *Tehillim* whenever the baby allowed to.

She remembers seeing Daniel being led into the courtroom in shackles and chains. The sight and the noise of the chains brought the awfulness of their situation to the forefront of her mind. Not allowed to speak to each other, they exchanged glances that spoke volumes. She held up their son so Daniel could see him, and Daniel smiled. That simple act of seeing his son seemed to put Daniel, for a moment, in a better frame of mind. Perhaps those few seconds of feeling normal helped him cope with what was to come.

There were many people in the courtroom, as many cases were being tried that day. The decision that would determine their lives for the next several years was in the hands of three formidable-looking judges who sat in flowing robes at the front of the room in elevated chairs, overlooking everyone.

As an American, Miriam had forgotten that in France there is a presumption of guilt, and innocence was something that needed to be proved by your lawyer. Guilt presumed, the relationship between the *juge d'instruction* (the prosecutor) and the judges is close. They are, basically, on the same team. It is you, the defendant, and your lawyer, who are on the opposing team. The onus is totally on you to change what has already been decided: your guilt.

Miriam and Daniel had two lawyers who worked exceedingly closely on their case. The one who was representing them in court specialized in criminal cases. Hélèn was a young, attractive, exceedingly kind, confident, tenacious, strong woman. Miriam had never seen her nervous — until that day.

This woman had had to fight to rise to her position in this male-dominated profession. But the French system, with its predetermined guilty sentence, forces the lawyers to be subservient and overly polite when presenting their case to the judges, almost groveling before the judge — at least that's how it appeared to Miriam — in order to get the best outcome for their client. Miriam had never seen her lawyer show so much deference to anyone. She measured every word carefully, clearly concentrating on each word used. Seeing this change in her lawyer terrified Miriam.

When Miriam was a young child, she would fall asleep whenever she was frightened. As she got older, she would force her mind to wander whenever she found herself in scary situations. The day of the trial was no exception. Barely understanding what was being said, Miriam told me she thought about how much preparation she and Daniel had put into this day, spending time on how they dressed, rehearsing what was to be said, and examining carefully every detail of their behavior.

Her mind wandered and took her to thoughts of the Heavenly Court that we approach every day in our prayers. There we are judged by One who not only decides our future and every aspect of our lives, but who loves us and has a relationship with us — unlike the judges sitting in front of her. Despite this, she mused, we all tend, when we pray, to do it by rote, without feeling, not always dressing properly, not always being careful of how we speak, and not always giving 100 percent of our attention. She committed herself from that point on, whatever the outcome, to pray differently. To pray with full concentration, with love.

Her thoughts returned to the present. She nursed the baby often, as the lawyers instructed her to do, and then tried to get him to cry.

And then the trial was over. Miriam and her lawyer left the courtroom to wait just outside for the judgment.

Daniel was taken back to his cell under the courthouse to await transportation back to the prison. No words were allowed between them. They could only wave good-bye.

Despite his outer smile when they led him from the courtroom, his lowered head and slumped shoulders reflected his worry and fear. She wondered what he was feeling at that moment. He was so totally isolated. She at least would be with their son. The anxiety of not knowing what was next must have been torture for him as he now faced the possibility of his future alone, so far from home and family.

Miriam does not remember how long she waited in the hall of the Palais de Justice with her lawyer, but it seemed like forever. Hélèn could not stop pacing, her anxiety mirroring Miriam's.

Miriam was afraid to allow herself to hope for a good verdict, yet more frightened not to. She wanted to go home so badly. How many times had she fought the desire to take her baby and run? But what about Daniel? What if she was able to go home with her baby but Daniel was sentenced? When would he see his baby again? How would they deal with the loneliness, the isolation, the pain, and the worry if they were condemned to live apart? How would she raise her child in a prison cell if she was sentenced? Every alternative possible, except freedom for them both, would be unbearable.

Miriam vaguely remembers an official finally coming and talking to her lawyer at length. She had no way of understanding what they were saying. Then her lawyer grabbed her hand and insisted they leave the

Palais de Justice immediately!

They went home, made arrangements, and packed up, and Miriam and the baby left France for good. Fearing the prosecutor had succeeded, again, in overturning the verdict, Miriam looked over her shoulder constantly. She continually imagined the police and the prosecutor running after them, apprehending her, and forcing her and the baby back to prison.

It was not until she took her seat on the plane and the wheels actually left the ground that she began to accept that she and her son were going home. Not until she landed in the country of her birth and the city she grew up in would she stop looking over her shoulder and begin to feel freedom.

Daniel, though, had been given a three-year sentence.

72
Journey Home

Everything happened so quickly that we only knew she was coming. We had no flight information. Miriam had to change planes several times and pass security often as she entered and left different countries on her way home. At each stage she could be delayed, miss her flight, and have to rebook. And so we waited by the phone to hear which plane would take her through the last leg of the journey and into our arms.

With just one more plane to catch, she stood on line for security, customs, and immigration. Once through those doors she would be on home soil and have just one more plane ride, a short two-hour flight to our home. She was tired and the baby was cranky.

But the immigration officer had concerns. The officer wanted to make sure the baby was hers. Miriam was delayed and questioned. Why was the baby's last name on his passport not the same as hers? Where was the father? Why had he not given written permission for her to take the baby home? How could they contact him?

Flashbacks of the last time she had endured questioning by an airport authority, which had led to jail and then prison, made her heart race and skin crawl. Would they, after all this, apprehend the baby? How could she prove she wasn't kidnapping her own child — whose last name was different from hers (since her passport still said her maiden name) and whose passport came from a different country?

She stood a few feet from the door that would lead her home and to safety; yet, as they continued to question her, it seemed like miles away. Without realizing it, she held her son tighter than was necessary. Miriam closed her eyes and prayed that G-d give her the right words to convince them to let her walk through those doors with her baby, through those doors to freedom.

Forcing herself to remain calm, believing that G-d had not allowed her to come this far for nothing, she chased the images from her mind, banishing memories of authorities who handcuff you and take away your freedom. She answered all their questions calmly. G-d had given her the right words. Finally, they let her through. Home at last.

There was only one seat left on the next plane that would bring her home — really home. She ran to catch her flight: they had agreed to hold the plane for her, if she hurried. She had been given the dreaded middle seat, between two large businessmen. Saying no to that seat would mean a five-hour delay. All she wanted at this point was to get home.

As she entered the plane with her screaming baby, she felt that everyone was looking at her. Many showed disdain, perhaps thinking that this young girl should have been more careful not to have held up the plane and make them all late. They all assumed the delay was her fault. Others just looked relieved that they would not be sitting next to a baby whose screams were larger than he was. The two businessmen looked clearly disappointed that they had not only lost the precious empty seat that was between them but would also have to contend with a screaming infant for two hours. But Miriam didn't care. She was going home.

Reuben and I waited anxiously at the airport. We had gotten there very early. Once we knew her flight information, there was no way we would risk being held up in traffic and not being there when she came off that plane. I had not seen her or the baby in months. And so we waited and waited for her to arrive. I found myself pacing, not even realizing what I was doing. Reuben and I spoke little, each of us lost in our own thoughts. Suddenly she was there in front of us.

I threw my arms around my daughter. I kissed her and kept touching her face to make sure she was there and was real and that this was not merely the scenario I had imagined so many times. I kept staring and hugging and could not let go, fearing she would disappear again.

Finally, she simply said, "Please, let's go home."

73
Longing for Normalcy

O ver the next several months we developed a routine. Everyone longed for a feeling of normalcy. And so, we made our life normal. We ate dinner together, took the baby for walks and to the park, taught him to reach for things, helped him learn to crawl, and applauded when he stood for the first time, just like any normal family would.

After a period of time that allowed Miriam to recuperate, she got a job as a babysitter. The family had no problem with her bringing her own child along. She loved the children she cared for. Her life was beginning to have purpose and meaning again, and the money she earned, though not a great deal, started to give her back a feeling of independence. She signed up for a hairdressing course at the local community center and began to comb wigs and give haircuts. These were the types of jobs that most people complained about, being tedious and low paying, but Miriam was overjoyed to be paid something and provide a service to others. She felt productive and proud of her work.

I saw the old Miriam returning as she began, one step at a time, to put her life back together. But Daniel was missing, and she was missing Daniel. As normal as life might have looked to outsiders, as normal as we tried to pretend it was, we all knew that Miriam could not, once again, be the person we had known until her husband returned.

Each Sunday we called in to Radio Shalom, a radio talk show in France that the prisoners, and Daniel, made sure to listen to. While Miriam spoke to the moderator on any topic so that Daniel could hear her voice, I tried to get the baby to gurgle or laugh so that Daniel could hear his voice. It was our hope that this contact with his family would give Daniel some solace and connection. We never missed a Sunday.

I was concerned about the baby being able to bond with his father after not seeing him for so long. It pained me to realize that Daniel would miss the whole first year of his son's life and maybe more. I printed up pictures of Daniel and placed them everywhere in the crib and hung them all over the baby's room. I prayed that this would help. My wish was that when they finally reunited, Daniel would be a familiar sight to his son and their relationship would progress easily.

We fell into a routine. The baby's first birthday came and we made him a lovely birthday party that included most of our friends as guests, but we knew the room should have been filled with other young babies and their parents. Despite this, everyone enjoyed the party as best they could — especially the baby, who received so many gifts. Daniel's absence was the elephant in the room, always present though never mentioned.

74
Post-Traumatic Stress

We often think we have passed a trauma and have gone on with our lives, but it's not until we find ourselves in a similar situation and react normally that we truly know if we have healed. Almost a year after Miriam's return, Daniel's family wanted her to attend a family wedding. She had been very hesitant to do any traveling and adamantly refused to accompany me on my frequent cross-border trips. The thought of even speaking to a customs agent brought back nightmares.

Daniel's family flew her and the baby to the wedding. No country's borders were crossed and Miriam coped well with the flight. However, when she went to board the return flight, the agent could not find her name on the passenger list. She had her boarding pass, but somehow her name had simply been omitted.

The agent called over his supervisor for assistance. Not being able to solve the problem, that supervisor called his supervisor. And though Miriam knew, rationally, that she was not in any trouble or danger, she started to sweat and shake and have flashbacks to the moment she had been pulled off the plane in France.

Whether fearing that this young woman with a baby might collapse or due to the fact that the boarding pass was in order — or maybe it was all simply divine intervention — they finally let Miriam on the plane. It took what seemed like hours before Miriam stopped shaking and calmed down.

That was the last time she flew for a long while. Clearly the healing was not complete. I wondered if it ever would be.

75

The Surprise Call

The seasons passed, the snow began to fall, and Miriam and the baby needed winter clothes, so we spent a Sunday shopping in the mall. Reuben tolerates shopping as long as he has a good book. All the better if there's a good bookstore in the mall. We all packed into the wheelchair-accessible van.

By the time we got to the mall, the baby was comfortably asleep in his car seat. Reuben told us he'd babysit — hopefully we wouldn't be too long, and besides he had a new book to read and a bottle for the baby. We left Reuben, his book, and our sleeping grandchild in the van, and off Miriam and I went to shop. We came back and checked on them periodically in case we were needed.

Almost a year had passed since Miriam had come home. We had no idea how much longer Daniel would serve time. Your sentence was reduced if you learned French, so Daniel signed up for French lessons in the prison. You could be reprieved and freed on certain holidays — that freedom usually did not extend to those who had committed crimes involving drugs, but it might. Your sentence would be reduced for good behavior. But reduced by how much? We didn't know. So

Daniel participated in everything he could to get out early. Neither we nor the lawyers knew when that would be. We prayed each day that it would be soon.

Reuben was one of the few people to own a cell phone at the time — a rare item back then. He had received it from the MS society in our city, having applied for a complimentary cell phone that the society was awarding to people who had multiple sclerosis and showed a need for one. Since Reuben continued to teach at the university, drove the accessible van, and was also a community rabbi, the society felt he was an appropriate candidate, and he was awarded a cell phone. Miriam and I did not have cell phones, though, so its use to us was limited.

Miriam and I were returning to the van with several packages, the shopping trip successful, when we were very disturbed to observe from a distance Reuben pacing outside the van in his wheelchair. As we approached, we saw him wheel himself to the corner, look down the block furtively, come back to the van, and then proceed in the other direction and do the same thing. At first we thought something was wrong with the baby. We ran toward the van.

"I've been trying to find you!" yelled Reuben. "I've called every store I could think of in the mall, asking if anyone looking like the two of you were there. I've been going crazy!"

My mind immediately regressed to crisis mode. Close to panic but forcing myself to sound calm, I asked what was the matter.

"Daniel's out! He called! He's being escorted to the airport and out of the country. He's on his way home!"

We had no further information. No flight number, no estimated time of arrival, no preparation. We had so many questions, but there was no way to reconnect with Daniel. They had allowed him to call, and when no one was home, he thankfully remembered Reuben's cell number. He had hoped to finally speak to Miriam, but that was not to be. He said he would call again when he landed. We didn't know when that would be. We didn't even know where they were taking him. We ran home and waited by the phone.

76
Flight to Freedom

When Daniel finally completed his sentence, he was required to leave the country immediately. He wasn't allowed to just walk out on his own and come home. Instead, he was ordered to remain in a holding area under supervision until he could be provided with two armed guards who would accompany him. Handcuffed and shackled, he was escorted to the airport. There, he and the guards boarded a plane that would take him back to his hometown. Once there, he would be handed over to local authorities before being freed, which could take a while.

And so Daniel found himself flanked on either side by two guards. Not terribly excited about having to make a long plane ride and an immediate return, they chained Daniel to his airplane seat and settled in for the duration of the flight.

Daniel, however, was overjoyed. After twenty-one months in prison, he was finally heading home. He could not wait to see his wife and baby. It had been almost a year since their last visit. His only contact with his family had been the letters we all continued to shower him with and the weekly Radio Shalom broadcasts.

I have never been on a flight that transported a convict. I wonder what people thought as they kept their distance from the man chained to his seat. Daniel must have felt awful as those around him eyed and judged and found him guilty once again.

Bad weather caused the plane to be diverted. Because of this, when the plane finally landed, there were no local authorities waiting. Daniel's French guards decided to simply let him go. He exited the airport and embraced freedom — finally, after almost two years of imprisonment.

Daniel grabbed a Greyhound bus and made his way to his parents' home. His next stop was to travel the long distance to our home, where his wife and baby were anxiously awaiting his arrival.

Daniel had been with violent people for almost two years. I remember on one of my visits with him, he asked me to bring him gloves that covered his hands but left his fingers free. In the prison yard, he often played Backgammon with an older prisoner. The weather was cold and these gloves would allow him to continue to play while keeping his hands warm.

Daniel told me, with eerie calm, that this man had been convicted of killing his wife with an axe. I was shocked that Daniel was hanging out with someone so vicious. But Daniel just explained that he was really "the nicest guy" who must have been driven to kill as "an act of passion." I wondered and feared for his new normal, and if it would reflect on whom he had become, now that he was out. Frankly, it frightened me.

I tried to remind myself that he had been in prison, not day camp. His prison was known for its aggressive offenders. My daughter's prison had been considered even more violent, yet she came out of it without having adopted any brutal tendencies. But she had only been incarcerated for four months. Almost two years of associating with violent behavior might be very different.

I remembered how, in December, the prison allowed the families to bring Christmas food packages. We bought Daniel all sorts of kosher treats, from deli to candies, and packed them carefully, making sure they didn't exceed the weight limit allowed.

Seeing an opportunity to improve his kosher food supply, Daniel got several of his fellow inmates who didn't celebrate Christmas or have family in France to request family food packages from us. There was an Abdullah, a Mohammed, and about ten other Arabs for whom we packed and delivered kosher food. Daniel then exchanged, as previously agreed, cigarettes for their kosher food packages.

Of course, the guards knew exactly who the goodies were for, and most smiled when I gave them my family gift package for Mohammed and the many others. Some guards, however, insisted on opening the package and weighing it. When one was overweight by a few ounces, they made me repack it and take out some of the food.

I was relieved to see the cooperation among Daniel and his fellow prisoners, instead of the daily violence I so feared. I hoped cooperation was more the norm.

That December Daniel ate well. But as I reflected on his prison company, I couldn't help but wonder if Daniel had changed. My daughter had been married less than a year when they left for France. How well did she know her husband? Would she be welcoming home someone who had now become aggressive? What would my daughter encounter the first time Daniel became frustrated or upset? Would the baby, who had begun to shun strangers, go to Daniel? Would they bond? If not, how would Daniel react to the rejection? Would he be the same humorous, caring person Miriam had married after witnessing daily violence?

I worried about this and other aspects of their readjustment to normal life. I worried if people would see them as guilty and refuse to trust them. Would Miriam and Daniel be able to pick up from where they had left off as productive members of their community? Would they ever be able to live normal lives again?

And so, the joy of Daniel's release was bittersweet. I prayed to G-d that He continue to see us through to the end.

77
Full House

hen we knew Daniel was arriving, Reuben and I went away for the day. We wanted to give the little family some time to become reacquainted, just the three of them.

By the time we returned, we knew my fears had been unfounded. The pictures of Daniel that I had hung in the crib and around the baby's room had accomplished what I had hoped. The baby flew into Daniel's arms and didn't want to leave him, *baruch Hashem*, and my daughter looked as radiant as she did the day of her wedding. Daniel greeted us in his usual joking manner. I whispered my thanks to G-d, who had taken care of us once again.

We settled into a routine. Miriam continued her job as Daniel readjusted to freedom. He and the baby accompanied her whenever possible. The adjustment had its highs and lows, its pleasures and pains, its ease and difficulties. Their daily routine had become rote and their normal almost no different from that of other young married couples.

Reuben and I knew that it was only a matter of time before they relocated. We lived in a small town with not many options for a religious young couple. As much as I would have loved for them to stay, I knew it wasn't realistic. We talked about their future. I suggested that they not return to the city they had left over two years before. There, they would always be the couple of notoriety and never be able to live a normal life. What I didn't know was how many people knew of their story, almost everywhere.

There is an expression, "*Mi ke'amcha Yisrael*, Who is like your nation, Israel"? Sometimes I, like so many others, forget how true this is. It usually takes adversity to remind us. Just as Miriam wrote from prison, we are one family. Jews, no matter their religious leanings, are siblings who care deeply about each other and the world. And when there is a need, they are always among the first to help.

I never knew who organized the fundraisers that took place in almost every major community that helped raise money for Miriam and Daniel's legal fees. I didn't even know these fundraisers were going on most of the time. People donated to my children without knowing who they were, just because they were in need. To be the recipient of tzedakah is very humbling. Most of us prefer to give rather than receive. But I cannot imagine how we would have managed the exorbitant expenses without their generosity.

78
A Parenthesis in
My Daughter's Life

A family celebration took Miriam, Daniel, and the baby to the city where they now reside. Within days — or perhaps hours — they fell in love with the community. Enamored of the togetherness, warmth, and caring nature of the residents, they decided to relocate. Daniel was offered a position that week, and so the decision was made by the time they had returned to our home.

The day they were due to leave, Daniel picked me up at work. He was so excited about the move, and I was excited for them. They had now lived with us and been dependent on us for almost a year, Miriam and the baby for much longer. Our schedule revolved around theirs and the house had been the normal noisy, busy place of a young, growing family. Soon they would begin life again as it should be. They would once again become independent and grow.

While driving home, Daniel turned to me and said, "Please don't be offended, but I'm so happy to be leaving."

I smiled and thought of the quiet that would soon return to my home. "Please don't be offended," I responded, "but I'm so happy you're leaving, too."

That evening another chapter of their life was beginning, while Reuben and I would be returning to a lifestyle we had been forced to abandon when all this began.

Miriam and Daniel quickly became respected members of their new community. Their door is always open to anyone in need. They rarely speak of what happened to them and live their lives as just another family – a large, comfortable, and happy family. Every time I visit, without fail, and see their healthy, growing family thriving in their warm home, I thank G-d for having allowed them to reclaim their lives. I am again overwhelmed with gratitude for His benevolence to us all.

A friend had called this horrific saga a parenthesis. It had a beginning and, she said, it would have a definite end. It was set aside from the rest of our lives, having something to do with it, yet separate, unrelated, and horrible, like a nightmare. And, thank G-d, the parenthesis has, indeed, finally closed.

79

Finding Forgiveness

I found out recently that Aaron had told Miriam before the trial
that it was okay to make a deal with G-d. He explained that
there were times throughout Jewish history that people made
commitments to G-d in an earnest desire to come closer to Him. G-d
might accept this and bring an end to the trouble they were drowning
in. Aaron suggested that Miriam take on a specific daily obligation and
ask G-d that she not be sent back to prison.

Miriam had always had difficulty saying the entire *Kerias Shema
Al HaMitah*. It is a long prayer, and she would often fall asleep in the
middle. Before the trial, Miriam committed to saying this prayer to
the end each night, asking G-d to show them mercy and let her take
her son home in its merit.

Miriam credits saying this *tefillah* every night, particularly the
preceding *"Ribbono Shel Olam,"* dealing with forgiveness, for her
ability to forgive those involved and move on with her life. This
included forgiving Daniel's former friend, who planted the drugs on
them.

This "friend" called them almost two decades after it all began to ask for their forgiveness. He called to apologize and said he was sorry.

Miriam answered the phone, not knowing who was at the other end. Daniel wasn't home. When he arrived home and Miriam told him about the call, he refused to return it. He said, "When he returns the first year of my son's life that he stole from me, then I may be able to accept his apology and forgive."

Fortunately, his "friend" didn't ask sincerely for forgiveness twice more and ask it directly from Daniel. According to Jewish law, sincerely asking for forgiveness and making a serious attempt to attain forgiveness three times, directly from the person you have harmed, obligates one to forgive. I don't know if Daniel could. Only time will tell, but the process of asking to be forgiven has not even begun.

Miriam's reaction was different. She told me that after the initial shock of discovering who was on the telephone (after so many years, she hadn't recognized his voice), she was surprised at how calm she was. She said "hi" and even asked how he was with honest sincerity, as if she was having a normal conversation. She commented to me later how impressed she was that he had found the courage to call and ask for their forgiveness.

She found herself surprised by her reaction. She didn't feel anger or rage, and the call really didn't upset her. Her biggest regret was not asking him why, after all these years, he felt compelled to call them to say he was sorry. She was curious as to his sudden motivation, but had no intention of calling him back to find out.

Miriam credits her saying that prayer every night with helping her realize that G-d is in charge. For reasons unknown to us, things are supposed to happen the way they do. She has come to realize that we are surrounded by miracles daily, from finding a parking spot to your children returning home from school safely each day. Miracles surround us, should we choose to see them. And if we recognize them and are therefore motivated to thank G-d for the care He encompasses us with daily, hopefully we will not need a wakeup call.

With the help of this *tefillah*, repeated nightly for fifteen years, she has learned to accept and forgive and go on and live with optimism. It has helped mold her into who she is and given her true freedom.

> *Master of the Universe, I hereby forgive anyone who angered or antagonized me or who sinned against me; whether against my body, my property, my honor, or against anything of mine; whether [he did so] accidentally willfully, carelessly, or purposefully; whether through speech, deed, thought, or notion; whether in this transmigration or another transmigration — I forgive every Jew. May no man be punished because of me. May it be Your will, Hashem, my G-d and the G-d of my forefathers, that I may sin no more. Whatever sins I have done before You, may You blot out in Your abundant mercies, but not through suffering or bad illness. May the expressions of my mouth and the thoughts of my heart find favor before You, Hashem, my Rock and my Redeemer.*

Today, when Miriam faces challenges big or small, her default is to ask G-d for help and to assist her in finding the right words and actions to deal with the situation. The commitment made fifteen years ago not only helped her then, but continues to be her beacon today.

Postscript

eople frequently comment on how fortunate we were to have such wonderful, positive support during the time of Miriam and Daniel's imprisonment. They are right. It is the support that enables you to get through the day. But that's not the whole picture. I just preferred to focus on the good and what was positive. Every situation brings both good and bad. But it's what you choose to focus on, to concentrate on, that fills your soul and helps you put one foot in front of the other so you can do what you need to do. Concentrating on the positive helps you make it through each day and each week, each month, and, if needed, each year until the end. Happiness is, after all, a choice.

We could have dwelled on that unknown woman who called our home a week into our saga and screamed at me because I was not yet in France with my daughter, paying her cousin hundreds of dollars to drive me around. Instead I smile as I think of the anonymous donor who helped with the expenses of getting my handicapped husband to France for the bris of our first grandchild.

I could have soured at the gentleman who used his prominence to get Miriam's phone number once she was released from prison, even though we apologetically refused to give it out to anyone. Not only would calls interfere with the host family's routine and our daughter's recovery, but having her whereabouts known was considered dangerous. I could have soured as he got the number and gave it out (despite our request not to) to the people whom he thought deserved it.

Instead, I choose to focus on my close friend who took the phone number at his insistence, put it in a drawer without a glance, saying that when she was told she could call Miriam — by us and not someone else — she would call her. And not a second before.

I could be angry at Miriam's neighbor who called and, despite my repeated protests to stop, kept telling me about her cousin, who delivered a deformed child in prison because of the lack of proper care. Instead I choose to remember how Tikva called me after each visit with Miriam, with positive words and stories of her health and upbeat state of mind. I focus on Tikva's special family who cared for Miriam and treated her like a sister. They gave refuge to our family and to my daughter before they even got to know us well. They visited Miriam in prison and took her laundry so she would not have to wash her clothes by hand. They cheered her with their visits, and were there for her throughout the whole ordeal, always caring, always giving.

I could, with fury, dwell on the derogatory term *goyta* that someone used when referring to the sister, noting that Miriam would be okay if she was sent back to prison, because the *goyta* would help her. Instead I fill my thoughts with this nun, the only one who spoke English in the prison. I remember how she helped Miriam learn the ropes. She got her stamps, pens, and paper right way, so she could finally contact us. She helped her get kosher food and got her maternity clothes when her other clothing didn't fit and my package of maternity clothes hadn't arrived. I remember how she helped us see Miriam on nonvisiting days, when the designated visiting days were on Shabbos or *yom tov*. Without her help during my first visit to France, I would only have been allowed to see my daughter four times and only half an hour each time.

The sister's weekly calls to us once we had returned home between our visits to France, telling us how Miriam was doing, were a lifeline. I focus on this nun and remember how a Lubavitch friend called the sister a *tzadekes* and reminded me how we see these tzaddikim, these righteous gentiles, in every religious group.

I could still be overcome with anger at all the people who asked us inappropriate questions, demanded information we were not free to give, and insisted they had a right to know. They felt we owed them answers to every question they asked because they had prayed for our kids. Instead I focus on the few who simply had one question: "Do I continue my prayers and psalms on their behalf, or are they no longer needed?"

I could cut off a relationship with the people who felt so free to say to me, "Come on, they must have known they were carrying drugs!" when I was beyond pain. Even if they felt that was true, I never understood how they could verbalize it to me! Instead I choose to remember the words of another, "For whatever reason G-d has determined they go through this, may it be over soon."

I could be unforgiving of a community leader who, in a very public format, gave false statements that did grave damage to their case. He had heard things about their story and repeated them without attempting to verify them or asking permission to do so, even though he corresponded with Miriam and Daniel frequently. Instead, I remember with utmost respect the people who asked us permission before any act they did, always putting my children's safety first. I choose to remember the people who, in a very private way, quietly and without fanfare, took care of Daniel and Miriam's physical and emotional needs, wanting nothing in return.

I could be incensed at the people who barely knew Miriam and Daniel, but who bombarded them with phone calls once they were free. They badgered them for information so they could brag to others of how they had spoken to the famous/infamous couple. Instead, I focus on my teaching assistant, a religious non-Jewish woman who would never lie. She continued to call me with support during the crisis, but insisted I tell her nothing about what was happening with my children. In case someone asked a question she was not free to answer, she wanted to be able to say honestly that she did not know anything.

I could be forever bitter and unforgiving at the betrayal of trust perpetrated by Daniel's longtime "friend" who gave them the drugs and started this nightmare. Instead I think of the dream team: three young men who were friends of Aaron and whom we didn't know who offered to help. And help they did! Their kindness and intelligence, combined with their youthful energy, left me humbled and feeling very blessed. And, of course, Aaron and his family, who did it all, helping, coordinating, and rescuing every step of the way. They sacrificed their time and put their family commitments on hold while they put it all together for us. Without them we would have been lost.

I could obsess over the prominent people who asked to become involved on the guise of being helpful and supportive. Perhaps they did think they were assisting and saw their own motivation as pure. But all I could feel was the self-serving nature of the "help" they gave. I could not discern any thought for my feelings and needs as I lost one of my few precious visiting days with my son-in-law so that their family members could visit in my place. There seemed to be no concern with all I was coping with when they yelled at me for being unable to find them convenient housing or, alternatively, host them in the tiny flat I had been loaned.

They sent visitors to the prison without telling Miriam or Daniel, never thinking of the fear that would cause them. Any attempt by me to explain the negative effects of their actions was met with a lecture implying my ingratitude. They never hesitated to tell me just how much they had given up in order to "help" and how grateful I should be for their unsolicited, unasked-for, and counterproductive efforts. I try to give them the benefit of the doubt and assume they meant well, despite the constant harm they did.

Instead of focusing on them, I try to concentrate on the kindness and thoughtfulness of the prison's Jewish chaplain, who saw Miriam every week and would fax us and let us know how she was. He constantly brought her kosher food packages to offset the delay of the kosher canteen order. These packages came with abundant emotional support and caring.

There were so many others who helped.

There was the woman who hosted my daughter and grandson for so many Shabbosos once they were out on bail but couldn't leave the country. Their bond became so close, deep, and long lasting that she crossed the continent recently to attend my grandson's bar mitzvah, as she had promised thirteen years before.

Daniel will never forget or be able to repay the rabbi who brought him his set of *Shas*, one volume at a time, so that Daniel could spend his time learning, both by himself and with the rabbi when he visited him in prison. Because of the regulations against book bindings, this rabbi removed the covers from each volume of his beloved set before bringing them to the prison. He insists on leaving them like that today, without the binding, so that he can remember the circumstance of what occurred and how the books were utilized.

There was the rabbi and so many others who helped raise money to assist with the legal fees. The family who sponsored Miriam's attempt at bail. Members of the French Jewish community who volunteered to help because they had experienced the coldness and isolation of the French prison system firsthand. The family who donated their spare office as an apartment for Miriam after the baby was born, and the lawyer who tracked them down for us when we had no idea where they were and thought they were dead.

He got them their first kosher meal in the jail. He also sent a courier to the prison when the fax machine was out of ink, so that they could sign on with him immediately and he could then begin working on the case without delay and find out what they had been charged with. He kept us informed and treated our children like family, only better. His partner specialized in criminal law. She was blunt, honest, a straight shooter who quickly became my daughter's "older sister," guiding her and caring about her with great warmth, a sense of humor, and a direct manner.

There was the family who welcomed Miriam when she was released on bail. They welcomed her as if she was a student coming to study instead of a convict they did not know. They trusted her, found her a doctor to deliver her baby, housed her and cared for her, and supported her in every way, physically and psychologically, throughout this ordeal.

I choose to focus on my memories of these people and their family and the memories of so many others in the French Jewish community who rallied and helped.

And, when I think about those times, I concentrate on the repeated miracles that had Miriam and Daniel convinced that though they could not understand why this was happening to them, they knew that G-d was holding their hands every minute.

I thank, with every fiber of my being, the selfless people of this story. People not of prominence or stature, but people just like you and me who wanted to help and who did help repeatedly and appropriately. Those people who asked with openness and honesty how to assist us and then listened to our answers. Our lives in France were enhanced so very much by the wonderful people who chose to get involved and lend support.

My daughter's experience has taught me never to underestimate what I can do to help others and not to just wait for those of stature or the large organizations.

My grateful memories of that time include reminiscences of my son. His support and humor were a true gift, a light in darkness, as he kept returning normalcy to a situation that was anything but normal. I remember how, during our first visit to Miriam in prison, he thanked her, with a wink and a hug, for making him "the good kid now." She winked back, returning the sweet feeling of normal sibling rivalry to our family, and we all laughed. Kids! My kids. Thank G-d.

Mostly I focus on my daughter, Miriam, for inspiration. She was twenty, pregnant and alone, but she found the strength to keep positive. She replaced negative thoughts with positive ones and turned horror into opportunity. Her faith, her generosity of spirit, and her caring of others remains as much a model for me today as it did fifteen years ago.

And so, I hope my daughter's letters and her story will help you, the reader, as you go through hard times in your own life. I pray that when you go through adversity, you take small steps. Take small steps always toward a goal, and focus, please focus, on the positive.

Glossary

Note: All terms are Hebrew unless otherwise noted.

ahavas Yisrael: Love of one's fellow Jew.

allez (French): Go.

am Yisrael: People of Israel, Jews.

amush: An acronym for *ad me'ah v'esrim shanah*, may you live till 120.

Ana BeKoach: A song filled with mystic significance whose lyrics are a prayer for Israel's redemption from exile.

Ani Ma'amin: A song based on one of Maimonides' Principles of the Faith. The words are "I believe with perfect faith in the coming of the Messiah, and even though he tarry I will await him each day."

Av: The name of a month of the Hebrew calendar, generally corresponding to August.

baruch Hashem: Blessed is G-d, an expression used to express gratitude to G-d.

bas mitzvah: A Jewish girl's celebration at age twelve of reaching adulthood.

bayis ne'eman b'Yisrael: A faithful home in Israel.

Beis HaMikdash: The Holy Temple.

berachah: Blessing.

b'ezras Hashem: With G-d's help, an expression used either in acknowledgment of G-d's past help or in prayer for help to come.

bitachon: Trust in G-d.

bris: Circumcision, the ritual surrounding the traditional surgical removal of the newborn's foreskin. This is the primary religious initiation of the male Jewish baby, normally done on the eighth day of life.

b'sha'ah tovah: In a good hour, said about the upcoming birth of a child.

b'sha'ah tovah u'mutzlachas: In a good and successful hour.

Bubby (Yiddish): Grandma.

Chabad: A Hassidic Jewish group, also known as Lubavitch, or, informally, a member or members of the group.

chalav Yisrael: Literally, Israelite milk, referring to milk that is supervised from milking to final packaging to ensure that no milk from a nonkosher animal be added.

challah: Traditional loaves of bread eaten on the Sabbath.

chizzuk: Strengthening, support, and encouragement.

cholent (Yiddish): A stew-like dish that is traditionally served on Saturday after being cooked overnight.

Chumash: The Pentateuch, the first five books of the Hebrew Bible.

daven (Yiddish): To pray.

davening (Yiddish): Praying.

divrei Torah: Plural of *d'var Torah*.

d'var Torah: Words of Torah, religious teachings.

Eichah: The Book of Lamentations.

emunah: Faith in G-d.

Even HaShesiyah: The Foundation Stone under the Holy Temple in Jerusalem.

erev Shabbos: Literally, Sabbath eve, referring to Friday before the onset of the Sabbath.

frum (Yiddish): Religious.

galus: Exile.

goyta (Yiddish): Literally, a non-Jewish woman, a term that has come to have a derogatory connotation.

Hashem: Literally, the Name, used by religious Jews to refer to G-d, whose other names are considered too holy for casual use.

hechsher: A rabbinical certification of kashruth, most often for food meeting the standards of Jewish law.

im yirtzeh Hashem: If G-d desires it; G-d willing.

interdit (French): Forbidden.

Iyar: The name of a month of the Hebrew calender, generally corresponding to May.

kadosh: Holy.

kallah: Bride.

Kerias Shema Al HaMitah: The Shema prayer and its accompanying paragraphs, recited before bedtime.

kesubah: A marriage contract signed at all Jewish weddings assuring the wife material resources in case of dissolution of a marriage by death or divorce. It also affirms the commitment of the partners to treat each other with mutual respect. Living as husband and wife is forbidden without the *kesubah*.

Kiddush: Prayer of sanctification recited at the evening and midday meals on the Sabbath and festivals and usually said along with the appropriate blessings for wine, bread, or liquor.

Kitzur: Short for *Kitzur Shulchan Aruch*, a handbook of Jewish law.

kohen: A male descendant of Aaron the High Priest, accorded special honor in Jewish law.

lailah tov: Good night.

lashon hara: Derogatory speech, speaking negatively about people. Such talk is forbidden by Jewish law.

leichter (Yiddish): Candelabra, often referring to those used to light candles in honor of the Sabbath or holidays.

Levi'im: Male descendants of the tribe of Levi, according special honors in Jewish law.

Lubavitch: A Hassidic Jewish group, also known as Chabad; or informally, a member or members of this group.

maariv: The evening prayer service.

malach: An angel.

mandat cash (French): Money order, a formal way to deposit money for use by prisoners.

Mashiach: The Messiah.

Mattos-Masei: Names of portions of the Torah.

Megillas Rus: The Scroll of Ruth, read on the holiday of Pentecost (Shavuot).

mekarev: Literally, bringing close, referring to outreach work or seeking to bring alienated Jews back to traditional practice.

middos: Character traits.

minchah: The afternoon prayer service.

mitzvah: A commandment. Colloquially in Hebrew and Yiddish, a good deed.

mitzvah tantz (Yiddish): A dance done in certain circles by the bride and her father at the end of a wedding.

Mizmor LeDavid: A reference to Psalm 23, which begins with these two words.

mohel: One who is trained in ritual circumcision.

mohelim: Plural of *mohel*.

neiros: Candles, usually referring to candles that are lit to celebrate the onset of the Sabbath and holidays.

nes: Miracle.

neshamah: The "breath" or spirit of a person, a soul.

neshamaleh (Yiddish): Little soul.

neshamos: Plural of *neshamah*.

nisayon: Trial, test of faith.

nosh (Yiddish): Treats, snack foods eaten for pleasure.

Omer: A period of time from the second day of Passover to the holiday of Pentecost, marked daily as a countdown to the giving of the Torah.

ovdei Hashem: Servants of G-d, obedient to His will.

Palais de Justice (French): Literally, "Palace of Justice," this is among the oldest surviving buildings of the former royal palace in Paris. Today it houses the justice of the state, as well as several other buildings.

parashah: The weekly Torah reading from the Five Books of Moses. The Torah is divided into sections each one of which is read, in whole or part, as part of prayer services on Monday, Thursday, and Saturday.

parloir (French): Conference or visitation.

pas Yisrael: Bread whose baking has been supervised by Jews.

potches (Yiddish): Slaps.

pidyon haben: Ceremony for the redemption of a firstborn son.

Pirkei Avos: Literally, Chapters of the Fathers, this is a tractate of the Mishnah which deals with conceptual and ethical issues.

posek: A rabbi who is a religious authority.

rabbanim: Plural of *rav*.

rav: Rabbi, traditionally a certified expert in certain fields of religious law.

refuah: Recovery, healing.

Rosh Chodesh: The first day of each Jewish month. Some months are thirty days long, in which case the thirtieth day is called Rosh Chodesh as well as the following day (i.e., the first day of the new month).

Rosh HaShanah: The Jewish New Year, a day of penitence and prayer. Its major ritual is the sounding of the ram's horn.

rosh yeshivah: The dean of a rabbinical or Talmudic academy.

ruchniyus: Spirituality.

sandak: The person honored with holding the baby at his circumcision.

sefarim: Plural of *sefer*.

sefer: A book, most often referring to a book of religious significance.

Sefer HaChinuch: A medieval work listing and defining the 613 biblical commandments.

sefirah: Literally, counting, referring to the counting during the Omer period, from the second day of the Passover holiday until the festival of Pentecost forty-nine days later.

segulah: An amulet or a spiritual or mystic element leading to a certain outcome.

seudas mitzvah: Festive meal held in honor of a religious ritual or lifecycle event.

Shabbat shalom: A peaceful Sabbath.

Shabbat shalom u'mevorach: A blessed and peaceful Sabbath.

Shabbos: The holy Sabbath, which begins each week at twilight on Friday and ends at nightfall on Saturday. It is traditionally a day of rest when many specific activities are forbidden.

Shabbosdik (Yiddish): Of the Sabbath or sharing the nature of the Sabbath.

Shabbosos: Plural of Shabbos.

shacharis: The morning prayer service.

shalom: Peace.

Shavuos: Pentecost, the Jewish holiday commemorating the giving of the Torah, also called Shavuot.

she'eilah: A question asked of one's religious authority.

sheitel (Yiddish): A wig. A Jewish married woman's hair is to be covered in mixed company. This can be done with a hat, scarf, or wig.

Shema: The first word of a biblical verse, "Hear O Israel, the L-rd is our G-d, the L-rd is One." It is the declaration of faith and acceptance of G-d as Master and His commandments as binding and begins a core section of morning and evening prayers.

Shir HaShirim: Song of Songs, recited by many on Friday night.

shivah: Literally, seven, referring to the seven days of mourning observed after the death of an immediate family member.

Shivah Asar B'Tammuz: The seventeenth day of the Hebrew month of Tammuz, observed as a fast day and a day of mourning over the breach in the walls around Jerusalem prior to the destruction of the Holy Temple and the exile of the Jewish people.

shluffy (Yiddish colloquialism): Sleep.

shofar: A ram's horn used as part of the special ritual of the Jewish New Year, Rosh HaShanah, it calls the Jew to repent. It is also blown to signal the end of the penitential fast of the Day of Atonement.

siddur: Jewish prayer book.

simchah: Joy, happiness, and any event or happening that generates joy and celebration.

Simchas Torah: The final day of the holiday of Tabernacles, a day of celebration of the completion of the yearly cycle of Torah reading.

snood (English): A cloth head covering.

Ta (Yiddish colloquialism): Dad.

tallis: A prayer shawl worn by married Jewish males.

Tammuz: The name of a month on the Hebrew calendar, generally corresponding to the month of July.

Tanach: The Hebrew Bible, which consists of three sections: Torah, the Five Books of Moses; *Nevi'im*, the books of the former and latter Prophets; and *Ketuvim*, holy writings, the remainder of the biblical writings, including such books as Psalms, Ecclesiastes, Chronicles, etc.

tefillah: Prayer.

tefillin: Phylacteries, worn by Jewish men during morning prayers.

tefillos: Plural of *tefillah*.

Tehillim: The Book of Psalms or the individual chapters of Psalms. These poetic sections have come to be used as a means of devout study and prayer in times of sickness, danger, or other special concerns.

Three Weeks: The period of time from the Seventeenth of Tammuz to Tishah B'Av, a period of mourning in the Jewish calendar.

Tishah B'Av: Literally, the Ninth of Av, the saddest day on the Jewish calendar, marking the destruction of both Holy Temples.

Torah: The Law, Divine Revelation, the Five Books of Moses, the Oral Tradition, or, by extension, the totality of Jewish law.

treif (Yiddish): Literally, torn; generally used to refer to nonkosher food items.

tzaar: Pain, trouble.

tzaddikim: Righteous individuals.

tzadekes: A righteous woman.

tzaros: Troubles.

tzedakah: Charity.

tzitzis: The colloquial term for a four-cornered garment traditionally worn by Jewish males.

vach nacht (Yiddish): A gathering that takes place the night before the circumcision ceremony. Prayers and learning surround the baby for protection.

vort (Yiddish): Literally, a word, also referring to a Torah discourse.

yahrtzeit (Yiddish): Anniversary of a person's day of death.

yeshuah: Salvation.

Yiddishkeit (Yiddish): Judaism.

yom tov: Literally, a good day, generally referring to biblical festivals such as Passover, Tabernacles, and Pentecost.

Zaidy (Yiddish): Grandpa.

zemiros: Songs traditionally sung at the Sabbath and holiday tables.

About the Author

*A*nn Novick was born and grew up in Brooklyn, New York. She has lived in the United States and Canada. With an advanced degree in special education, she has spent her working career helping young children achieve their potential and successfully integrate in the regular classroom.

Ann began writing professionally when her husband became chronically ill, early in their marriage. Her column, "The Person behind the Chair and Beyond," has been published weekly in the *Jewish Press* for over ten years. It shares the common experiences faced by spouses of the chronically ill in order to heighten awareness.

Behind Prison Walls is her first book.